TEACHING IN THE POST COVID CLASSROOM

Mindsets and Strategies to Cultivate
Connection, Manage Behavior and Reduce
Overwhelm in Classroom, Distance and
Blended Learning

GRACE STEVENS

Red Lotus Books

Also by the Author:

Positive Mindset Habits for Teachers - 10 Simple Steps to Reduce Stress, Increase Student Engagement and Reignite Your Passion for Teaching

Positive Mindset Journal for Teachers (3 editions)

The Happy Habit: 10 Simple Habits - Step By Step Guide To Finding More Happiness & Joy in Your Life

Mindfulness Meditation for Beginners: From Zero Ten in Ten - A No-Nonsense Starter Guide for Seekers and Skeptics

Stop Procrastinating: 9 Simple Habits Step By Step - How to Regain Control of Your Time and Your Life in One Fun Filled Week

Praise for Teaching in the Post Covid Classroom

"Having taught at just about every level from early primary to university students over the last 50 years, I am amazed at how much I learned from Grace Stevens' new book... Each page is packed with sound ideas and straightforward approaches to engage students and inspire teachers! This book should be required reading for every teacher in order to embrace the "new normal."

Cindie Fisher - Veteran Teacher

*"Stevens balances the art of maintaining a friendly and conversational tone while staying **succinct with her advice on how to create a challenge-proof classroom culture.** Intertwined with vulnerable personal stories and lessons-learned, I'm sure many teachers will find themselves empathizing with her experiences and **finish the book feeling more empowered to tackle this new school year.** No matter what surprises it holds."*

Frankie Robinson - The Educator's Book Club Facebook Community and host of This is My Teacher's Voice Podcast

Dedication

*"So Matilda's strong young mind continued to grow, nurtured by the voices of all those authors who had sent their books out into the world like ships on the sea. These books gave Matilda a hopeful and comforting message: **You are not alone.**"*

From "Matilda" By Roald Dahl

Download The Free Workbook

Grab the Workbook and Journal Pages

TO GET the most out of this book, please print out and use the free 35 page workbook. It includes exercises, worksheet pages and a Bonus Section.

It is available for FREE download at http://happy-classrooms.com/workbook-ppc/

You can also download six weeks worth of the Positive Mindset Journal For Teachers that is the perfect place to practice your mindset habits.

If you are reading the digital version of this book, simply click the link below. If you are reading a physical version of this book go to:

http://happy-classrooms.com/workbook-ppc/

Contents

Part I

Part II

Preface

There Was No Drill For This

Do you know how many students have died in school fires in the last five decades? None that I could find. Even so, once a month, school children and teachers in the United States trek out to a playground or field to practice a fire drill. We have protocols for natural disasters, suspicious packages, and, regrettably, how to hide, flee, or fight in the event of an active shooter on campus. Every school has a thick safety binder laying out procedures for every possible dramatic contingency. Well, almost every contingency. No one in education planned for a world pandemic.

In the spring of 2020, with fears of the Covid-19 Coronavirus rapidly spreading, schools across the globe took the unprecedented action of closing campuses. With no notice and no training, teachers were tasked with providing instruction remotely out of their homes. We scrambled, we rallied, we got it done.

The long term social and emotional trauma of the extended shelter in place order on students is still to be determined. The academic fall out? Students had no previous experience in remote learning, and have never had to deal with social isolation. It's unlikely they were doing their best learning. Moreover, I've yet to find a teacher that thinks their best teaching comes from behind a camera lens. For many educators, with their own children at home needing academic assistance and parental attention, it was survival mode at best.

I'm writing this in the summer of 2020, a historical time when the pandemic in the USA shows no sign of slowing down. Plans for the upcoming school year change daily. We owe it to our students and ourselves to move beyond survival mode.

Now is a time for a reboot. A time to step back and be more strategic and proactive. A time to reflect and construct instructional plans and practices that will be effective and sustainable moving forward. We need support and resources to help teachers adjust, and maybe even learn to thrive, in this new educational environment.

What schools returning will look like is still being debated. Politicians, administrators, and union leaders are negotiating how to safely and efficiently navigate reopening campuses while meeting the guidelines of the Center for Disease Control and Prevention.

Perhaps by the time you are reading this the directives such as mandatory face masks, desks 6 feet apart, running campuses and buses at 50% capacity in shifts, and no recess, assemblies, or cafeterias will all be things of the past. We can only hope. But we now live with the knowledge that it's possible to leave school on Friday, believing you were totally prepared for the following week with your objectives for Monday written on the board, only to learn an hour later that you will be providing instruction from home. It's happened before, it can happen again.

Regardless of when you find your way to this book, the strategies will still apply. While the apps and devices may have changed, the principles have not.

The information in this book will help you address these fundamental challenges of in class and online education:

- How do we manage behavior and accountability in class and remotely?
- How do we form a sense of community and collaboration between a group of students who we have maybe never even met?
- How do we create lesson plans and leverage technology to make sure we are not just using new tools to do "old work"?
- How do we stay energized in such a dynamically changing environment and avoid burnout?

The answer to these questions will be of benefit regardless of what the new teaching landscape looks like, whether we are delivering instruction from our teaching podium in class or our kitchen.

Introduction

When Teaching Brings You To Your Knees

I have an aversion to platitudes. Hearing cliches such as "Everything happens for a reason" or "Time heals all wounds," no matter how well-intentioned, lands like nails on a chalkboard. But in this instance, the platitude was true - life's gifts often come in strange packages.

The gift was a defining experience that led me to make a decision. That decision was to tune out the overwhelming external "noise" that had led me to become insecure about my teaching and to prioritize connection with my students over the curriculum.

Four months after I made this commitment to myself, the Coronavirus pandemic caused schools worldwide to unexpectedly close. Teachers were faced with the unprecedented challenge of delivering instruction for the rest of the school year from their homes. Many teachers struggled with having their students participate in distance learning.

The time I had invested in creating a strong classroom sense of community served me well. While our transition did have plenty of bumps in the road, we struggled far less than many other classes. The majority of students participated in our daily video conferences, all of them completed work and participated in our year-end project. We even had some fun along the way.

Our "shelter in place" experience confirmed my belief that even the most well-researched lesson plans, utilizing all the best bells and whistles that technology has to offer, are irrelevant if students don't show up to work on them. The experience that led me to make that decision four months previously had been a gift that saved me.

So what was this defining experience? A motivational speaker? A student whose life I turned around? Nothing quite as romantic as that. Remember, it came in a strange package.

I could say I was experiencing an existential teaching crisis where I was confronting important questions.

"Are we equipping students with the skills they need to compete in the 21st-century global economy, or simply teaching to the test?"

"Am I succeeding in my role in cultivating a culture of self-motivated learners?"

But the reality was a lot less dignified. It involved me curled in the fetal position, loudly sobbing during my lunch break. Afraid of being stumbled upon by my coworkers or, worse, my students, I was hiding in the only place I could be assured of solitude - a crowded supply closet.

Now I faced a dilemma. Would I be able to hear the bell in the closet? Would a line of children be abandoned on the playground when lunch was over? So, I did what any sensible teacher would do. I indulged myself five minutes of hysteria then got up. I washed the mascara streaks off my face. I greeted my students at the door with sun glasses and a forced smile. I announced they had worked so hard in the morning they'd earned another 10 minutes of recess, buying myself just enough time to stop hyper-ventilating. Hardly the stuff of Mr. Holland's Opus.

Many new teachers have found themselves equally drained and over-whelmed. More than forty percent of teachers abandon their careers within the first five years. But I wasn't a new teacher. I was eighteen years into my career in education. I was also four months into what I had considered to be my dream teaching assignment. I was working with a team of passionate, professional, and progressive educators. The students were well behaved and high achieving. The district was well funded and had every resource you could imagine. The school was walking distance from my house. What more could I want?

I had underestimated the toll of working with an entirely new curriculum, technologies, and student demographics. I was exhausted, overwhelmed, and experiencing a severe case of culture shock. Worse, I lived in a constant state of anxiety. I had come from a tiny school district where teachers had a lot of creative liberty. Now, everything from what was written on the board to what I said and how students engaged in academic discourse was highly scripted. I had come from an environment being tenured, well respected, relaxed, and totally focused on student needs and learn-ing. Now, in an award-winning district where I needed to prove myself all over again, I was adopting a teaching style that I thought administrators wanted to see. The district was very high performing, which is great. But high performing also meant high pressure and extremely data driven.

I had bought into the false narrative that the teams of people descending on my classroom with clipboards were there to catch me doing something wrong, not to facilitate professional development. What I was doing didn't feel authentic, as if I had adopted a fake accent. I was disconnected from my students, and I knew it. Nothing about my teaching felt inspired, creative, or really engaging. It's as if my class and I were going through the motions, checking all the boxes without really synergizing or bringing out the best in each other.

The relatively benign incident that led to my lunchtime retreat to the supply room was a student asking a question. Not an impertinent or off-topic question, just a question about what we were studying. In my frenzied rush to hurtle toward the next mandatory learning objective, I groaned we didn't have time for questions. That's right, kids! No time for curiosity, for engagement, for the magic that happens when the class meanders down a path of interest that leads to a "teachable moment."

The student didn't seem to care too much about my reaction, but I felt frustrated and ashamed. We all deserved so much more. And as the only adult in the room, it was up to me to deliver it. My stress was exasperated by the fact that I was awaiting results of several medical tests and a biopsy. The reality that I might have cancer or need to take the rest of the year off to attend to my health was looming over me. Surely this would not be my teaching legacy?

For some reason, the words of a quirky professor in my credentialing program almost two decades before came back to me. We'll get to him and those nine words later in the book. For now, it's enough to know that those words reached into my teacher's heart and encouraged and empowered me. I made the decision to stop being scared. I committed to investing in the things I know for sure make a difference in the classroom. I vowed to find my way back to being a teacher I would want for my children, the teacher my students deserved, and the teacher I knew I could be. My embarrassing meltdown had been a career saving gift. Cue rousing soundtrack!

This single breakthrough and mindset allowed me to persevere in a challenging teaching environment with my whole heart, and carve out a rewarding and positive classroom experience that helped preserve my sanity and boosted learning and engagement. When the pandemic struck, rather than being overwhelmed, I found myself (and my students) prospering far better than we had any right to be.

This book is meant to help you create your own challenge-proof classroom culture, so that your classroom and your teaching career are immune to massive upheavals, whether they be dramatic like a pandemic, or more mundane like an unscheduled observation the day after Halloween.

What You Will Learn in This Book

Although the concepts in this book are intricately connected, I divided it into three distinct sections for ease of structure and organization.

Section One: Mindset Matters

Teaching is not for the faint of heart. It can be both physically and emotionally draining and necessitates that we bring the best of ourselves to our students every day. There is no quick "positivity band-aid" that we can stick on the challenges and increasing demands of our profession to make it magically all better. But while "Attitude is everything!" may seem like a worn-out cliche (here come those nails on the chalkboard again), that doesn't mean it isn't true. There are intentional actions we can engage in to feel less stressed and more positively oriented. Plenty of research-backed data in the field of positive psychology exists to prove that. In compiling the strategies in this book, I combined my background in Neuro-Linguistic Programming, and 18 years of hands-on classroom experience. I chose the most helpful mindsets and easy to apply practices in this section to help you:

- Reframe the narrative we tell ourselves about education and teaching
- Practice mindsets that make us feel empowered and energized
- Develop intentional habits that enable us to focus on the positive aspects of our day
- Positively embrace the challenge of rethinking how we deliver instruction
- Define for ourselves our "teaching truths"

Section Two: Connection, Community, Consequences, and Curriculum

In this section, you will examine the core principles of what it takes for students to connect, engage, and learn. I outline how to effectively manage student behavior in the classroom and remotely. I identify the critical elements of a remote teaching plan, and how to start your year off strategically so that your students have the skills they need to work remotely if we ever have another year that takes a sudden plot twist.

You will learn how to:

- Develop a back to school plan that sets your class up for success
- Cultivate class community whether students are on campus, at home, or both
- Design an effective distance learning plan and be confident using the appropriate technology
- Eliminate busy work and prioritize curriculum that engages students
- Leverage technology to reduce tedious teacher tasks that take away from your real priority - connecting with students and helping them learn
- Construct an effective classroom management plan that minimizes power struggles and produces self-motivated students

Section Three: Overcoming Teacher Overwhelm

While all of the ideas in this book will help you manage teacher overwhelm, this section is where I share the best tactics to juggle all of your responsibilities and avoid burn out. These strategies will help you:

- Successfully navigate the stressful waters of how you are perceived as a teacher

- Learn how to tactfully set boundaries on your time
- Implement the most effective time management hacks to supercharge your productivity
- Utilize the science of peak performance to reclaim time to spend with your loved ones and interests outside of teaching
- Diagnose areas in your life that are out of balance
- Feel fulfilled as a teacher and reconnected to your passion

What This Book Isn't About

As someone who deals with the demands of this profession every day, I wrote a book that I would want to read. That means that I kept it as short and practical as possible. I minimized the academic jargon, steered clear of any acronyms, and did not include footnotes citing research. I added some useful resources at the end for further reading on the concepts I explore. The content is based on knowledge, experience, and a healthy dose of common sense.

The result is that this book should be easy to read and instantly applicable. However, it also means that its casual tone will likely not appeal to those looking for a more research paper type academic publication.

Also, this book is not a "how-to" guide on instructional technology. I am not a tech guru. I discuss the types of content management systems and communication apps needed to provide online or blended instruction and use examples of ones with which I am familiar. But there is no discussion of precisely how to use any software.

Once it became critical, I ramped up my knowledge of educational technology mostly thanks to a fantastic curriculum team, YouTube, and a few short online classes. My greatest tutors were actually my students. That in itself is a testament to the power of class community!

The focus is more on setting up a system that uses technology to deliver instruction that engages students without overwhelming them or their parents. While technology and apps may change moving forward, the principles will not.

Teaching is becoming increasingly more exacting. We understand why educators are leaving the profession at alarming rates. We need to find a better balance between the demands of our jobs, and our relationships and responsibilities outside of the classroom.

Not all days in teaching are going to be award-winning. Plenty of them will simply be "good enough." But if we are strategic in our planning and intentional about where we place our time and energy, we can have a positive and rewarding teaching experience. There is plenty of joy still to be found, whether we're connecting with students in a classroom, or through a screen.

Yes, teaching is challenging. But the ideas in this book will help.

Let's get started.

Part I

MINDSET MATTERS

1

Mindset Matters

Welcome to Holland

THERE IS a poem by Emily Pearl Kingsley called <u>Welcome to Holland</u>. It's a poem offering comfort to the parents of special needs children. Kingsley, who has a child with Down Syndrome, likens the excitement of preparing to be a parent to the excitement of preparing for a beautiful trip to Italy. We have planned for this trip, we are looking forward to so many things in Italy. Everyone is excited for us and the adventure we are undertaking. Then lo and behold, the plane lands in Holland, not Italy. Everything is different than we expected.

There's nothing wrong with Holland, we can still have a beautiful and rewarding vacation if we get over our initial disappointment. Kingsley's poem contends that we can learn and appreciate all of the beautiful things that Holland has to offer if we approach it with the right mindset.

Our abrupt detour into the land of distance learning (and more appropriately, distance teaching) felt a little like arriving in Holland. None of us imagined this when we signed up to be teachers. When we dreamt of being educators, the image we held in our minds was not that of us sitting at a computer all day, creating digital lesson plans, and only interacting with students over a screen. We anticipated moments of connection and laughter in the classroom, watching students collaborate and problem solve, and being engaged and excited. That magical moment when we observe a student grasping a concept they had been struggling with ... this was Italy and what we had spent years training for. It was what we were used to. We knew the language. Ramping up our knowledge of instructional technology, chasing down students to get work turned in, having a lot of that work be uninspired, or incomplete was not. Holland was seeming stressful and unfulfilling. The novelty of wearing pajamas to work and using the bathroom whenever we wanted quickly wore off.

When the original shelter in place orders got extended, and the reality that we would not be returning to campus for the rest of the year sunk in, there was a genuine grieving that occurred. In many ways, we had been cheated out of the best part of the year with our students. We didn't get to say goodbye or celebrate the end of the year the way we were used to.

Although many schools worked hard to creatively recognize graduating students, there's no denying that all students missed out on the anticipated rights of passage such as field days, proms, and award ceremonies. Our hearts hurt for our children and students who had worked so hard to get college acceptance. It became apparent that instead of having "rush week" and meeting new dorm roommates to look forward to, their first semester in college was likely to be a combination of physical distancing and online lectures. We were sad for them and for ourselves.

Many of us are still struggling to conceive of a "Back to School" where we cannot give hugs or high fives and where students need to maintain a physical distance and not touch the same objects. Classes and recess in shifts, not eating together in the cafeteria, no field trips, no small group collaboration. Will we be sucking the joy out of everything we love about school? No singing! Can students even see us smile through a mask?

I'll admit it, it's a bummer all the way around. There are no quick, positive affirmations that can make it all better. However, this is now our reality, for a while at least. We are in Holland. Taking time to grieve and gently hold space for what our students and we are feeling is important. But at a certain point, we need to pull out the new guide book and figure out how to make the best of Holland.

I am not a naturally optimistic person. I didn't inherit the "Let's make the best of it!" gene. But years of study and intentional practice in positive psychology have taught me habits that I can use to feel a lot better. In my book <u>Positive Mindset Habits for Teachers</u>, I quoted research from Harvard that only 10% of what makes us happy is a result of our actual circumstances. 50% comes down to our natural inclination ("glass half full" people). The other 40% can be dramatically influenced by intentional habits and mindsets we can practice to boost our natural happiness set point. So these suggestions are not just "wishful thinking," they are scientifically proven to help if we are intentional about practicing them consistently.

Focus on What You Can Control

Much of our stress comes from things beyond our control. Teachers and school administrators were never consulted or warned about the decision to suddenly close schools. Negotiating what future classrooms will look like is also out of our sphere of influence. Politicians, budgets, ever-changing guidelines from scientists and health officials all have their part to play. The situation is dynamic.

We also have a limited influence on students. When we are together in a classroom, we can control the environment and ensure everyone has equal access to what they need. When we participate in distance learning, we simply can't.

We have no control over students' physical circumstances and the inequity of their situations. Some have a personal device at their disposal, lightning-fast internet speed, a quiet area to work, and parents available to help them stay on task and complete their assignments. Others do not.

Apart from the digital divide, students may also be disadvantaged by food insecurity, a chaotic household, or the responsibilities of having to look after siblings as parents are either at work or trying to work from home.

We also have relatively little influence over the degree to which students participate and their work quality. It's not as if we can hold them in for recess to finish their work. The consequences we can enact to hold them responsible are limited. This causes teachers frustration. It is stressful to have responsibility for something without having much control over it.

So it's helpful to try and make peace with all of what we can't control, and focus on what we can.

We have control over the effort we put into our planning and our interactions. Depending on our situation, we might have more creative control over the curriculum and projects that we assign remotely. We certainly have control of our attitude and our energy.

One common theme in my work is the idea that our energy speaks louder than our words. Students are looking to us to see how to react to all of the new changes. When we initially thought shelter in place was only for a few weeks, I presented the situation to my students as a fun learning adventure! We'd figure out how to do it together. As the "adventure" stretched out, the novelty wore off and the fatigue and frustration set in, I still focused on bringing the best of myself to my students for the hour that we spent together daily. I still had control of the time of our daily meetings, even if I couldn't control who showed up to them.

Did I have students who didn't care about the quality of their work? Sure. Was it hard to track down parents and enlist their help in holding students accountable? Some of the time. But that's no different than being on campus. There will always be students and parents who have other priorities and, at a certain point, we need to concede that while we have some influence, plenty of aspects of teaching are beyond our control. Allowing them to cause us stress is not productive.

Assume the Best Intentions

"The most important decision we make in life is whether we believe we live in a friendly or hostile universe."

Albert Einstein

I believe that we live in a friendly universe. I assume people are doing the best they can with the skills that they have and within the situation in which they find themselves. I don't believe that anyone got out of bed this morning intending to purposely mess with my day.

The most productive mindset to adopt in these changing times is that people are acting with best intentions. The worldwide pandemic was a totally unprecedented situation for which there was no cohesive playbook.

Hopefully, we have all learned things that will help with similar situations in the future. But recognize that no matter how inconvenient or disruptive new school guidelines are, their purpose is to keep children and teachers safe.

While assuming the best intentions for the "big picture" decisions, it's also important to assume the best intentions within our daily interactions.

Try not to sit in judgment of parents who are not making what we perceive to be the appropriate effort in holding their child accountable. The reality now is no different than when children are in class with us. We never completely know the home situation that students are dealing with. Some households are in complete chaos with parents having lost jobs, or working from home while struggling to help their children.

Extend some grace to parents and assume that we all have the same goal of their child learning and succeeding. Older students who we feel should be more independent in their studies might be in charge of their siblings or have other responsibilities outside of schoolwork.

When I say extend a little grace to others, I mean to assume the best intentions and to be extra patient and understanding. Try not to take things personally.

Again, I don't believe that people purposely try to upset us. In reality, most people are focused on themselves and their own problems, not on others. Sometimes negative interactions are simply reflections of how their day is going. Just like we counsel students when helping them resolve conflicts, how other people treat us often says nothing about us and everything about them.

If people are impatient and unreasonable, try to feel empathy for them. Setting boundaries with people is important, but being defensive rarely helps.

Let Go of Comparison

Just as we extend grace to others, it is helpful to extend grace to ourselves. This is something I will explore further in the section on Overcoming Teacher Overwhelm. For now, realize it's best not to compare what you are doing to what other teachers are posting on social media. Remember, nobody is posting their lessons and projects that failed!

Many teachers had to scramble to put together a distance learning program. I am thankful for all the excellent tech-savvy educators who posted videos of how to make engaging slideshows and automate every aspect of their teaching. Before the shelter in place order, I had barely flirted with Google Classroom thinking, "That looks cool. I'll learn how to use it properly one day."

Well, when that day unexpectedly came, I relied heavily on those videos. Being frustrated at myself for not embracing Google Classroom sooner, or not having beautiful projects of my own to share wasn't productive. Remember, you are doing the best you can with the skills you have in the situation you find yourself in.

Don't fall into the trap of "Imposter Syndrome," believing that other people know more than you or are more qualified than you. We all have different strengths. The fact that you found your way to this book already means that you care enough to learn more and be the best you can be for yourself, your family, and your students. That's already a lot.

Let yourself off the hook if you feel you are struggling with new technologies and rules of engagement with students. Everybody's journey is going to look different. Remember the Growth Mindset posters on your classroom wall? Their message applies to teachers, too. We are learning and growing and modeling to our students that we can persevere and do difficult things.

Let Go of the Idea That Self Care is Selfish

Teaching is a helping profession. Most of us are natural caretakers and dedicate much of our time, energy, and passion to helping others learn and be successful. While it sounds like one of those cliches I don't like, it is accurate to say we can't pour water on others if our own vessel is empty. Establishing boundaries on our time and embracing routines that allow us to rest and replenish our energy are essential to teaching. There's a reason on airplanes we are told to put on our oxygens mask before attempting to help others. If we pass out, we are not useful to anyone else.

Whether we are teaching in the classroom or providing distance learning, our students and our families deserve the best of us. When we are exhausted and frustrated, we cannot effectively solve problems, and we are less productive. We begin to get resentful and unpleasant to be around. Taking care of ourselves isn't selfish, it's necessary.

I will explore specific strategies to help with this later in the book, but it all begins with mindset.

Rewrite the Narrative You Tell Yourself

"I have lived through some terrible things in my life, some of which actually happened."

Mark Twain

The story we tell ourselves matters. If we do not pay attention to what we are thinking, we let other people craft the narrative of a situation, and that narrative may or may not be accurate. In most cases, it will be fueled by fear and anxiety. I'm not being overdramatic when I say this. Mass media often has an agenda (hint, it's not to promote the idea that we live in a friendly universe). We are inundated with stories of conflict and trauma. Research in neurobiology reveals that of the 60,000 thoughts we have each day, approximately 90% are negative.

It is helpful to become aware of the story we tell ourselves, and to ask ourselves the simple question, "Is that really true?", "Do I have evidence of that?"

I'm not talking about conspiracy theories or anything extreme. I'm talking about the everyday stuff that we get ourselves all worked up about. For example, somebody in a fancy car cuts us off in traffic, and our judgment is off and running, assuming the person is selfish or arrogant and doesn't care about safety. We might make generalizations such as, "All people who drive that type of car are jerks or think they are better than the rest of us." Or we might make judgments on them based on their bumper stickers.

If we stick with the facts, the only thing we know is that the person cut us off. We have no idea why. Maybe they were distracted and didn't realize what they did. Maybe there's an emergency with a loved one, and they are stressed and rushing to get to a hospital.

Has this ever happened to you? You receive a message from a parent that they want to meet with you after school, and then worry about it all day? You assume there is some sort of problem, and waste a lot of time and mental energy rehearsing an imagined dialogue or confrontation.

I've been guilty of this so many times. I've made up a whole narrative and lived through the stress of it, and then nothing negative actually happened. The parent simply wanted to ask me a question or give me supplies for the classroom.

So what narrative are we telling ourselves about teaching? That's it's overwhelming and stressful? That there's no way to do everything we need to do and have an adequate work/life balance? That every teacher gets burnt out and is under-appreciated? That might be true of some teachers. But it's not true of all teachers. Other people's experience doesn't need to be our experience. We get to write our own narrative.

A turning point for me during the teaching breakdown I described in the introduction was when I decided to rewrite the story I was telling myself about my new position. First, I made a list of all of the positive aspects of it. It was a long list! Did I mention the school is walking distance from my house?

The other thing I did was write down the facts about my interactions with my administrator. Unfortunately, I had allowed myself to get sucked into the negative story that some others told about him and his management style. I felt I got along well with him and that he had a lot of positive attributes. However, I worried he really favored a rigid teaching style that felt very foreign to me. Others told me stories of him micromanaging and having unrealistically high expectations. No wonder I started feeling insecure and broke out in hives at the thought of him coming into my room unannounced!

I decided to get out a piece of paper and wrote down the "facts" (not opinions) about all of my interactions with him. On close inspection, there was nothing to back up the false narrative I had been told. I'm not saying that the story wasn't true for others, but it certainly wasn't true for me.

I realized that he was organized and had excellent follow through. He had been very responsive to anything I had asked of him, whether it was equipment or furniture or additional training. On the occasions when he did pop into my room unannounced, he seemed relaxed with the students and left a handwritten note in my box complimenting me on something he'd observed, or sent a quick email.

He was indeed very data-driven and a stickler for things being done in a very structured way. But I had learned more from him in a few months than I had in many years previously. He challenged me to grow and took the time to coach me in specific areas. My previous experience with administrators was always to hear, "Everything you do is great!" While it's so nice to get that feedback, it doesn't propel you to improve your craft.

When he announced he was moving to a director position in another district at the end of the year, I was very happy for him, but also a little disappointed for myself. I am so glad that I tuned out all of the external opinions that were stressing me out and allowed myself to have my own experience with him.

Again, other people's experience doesn't need to be your experience. You get to create your own.

Focus on What You Want, Not What You Don't

This process of writing down positive aspects is powerful. You may recall from basic psychology classes that human brains have a strong negativity bias. However, there are intentional habits we can practice to train our minds to be more positively inclined. Looking for positive aspects is one of the simplest.

I like to think of it in terms of being a detective, setting my radar to look for things that please me, and then taking mental note when I find them. In Positive Mindset Habits for Teachers, I talked about viewing being a "Joy Detective" as a game. Here's an example. When I leave my classroom to go to the staff room or make copies, I challenge myself to find five things that I like on the playground or campus. I make a mental note of things that please me during the day and write my three favorites down before I leave school.

It might seem too simple to be effective, but there is much research out there to support the idea of self-fulfilling prophecies. Confirmation bias is the term used to describe our brain's tendency to look for evidence to confirm what we already believe to be true. If we believe we are surrounded by hard-working, well-intentioned students and adults, then that's who we will notice. If we think everyone is a lazy rascal, that's who we'll notice, too. If we believe we got out of the wrong side of the bed and that everything that could go wrong in the day will indeed go wrong, then that will be our experience.

We get what we expect. Therefore, it's a productive habit to focus on looking for evidence of the things we want to experience, not the things we don't.

When I say focus, I'm not only referring to what we think about, I'm also referring to what we talk about.

Before heading into the staff room, I set my intention to focus on something positive or funny that happened in my classroom. That way, when I'm talking to other teachers, I'm sharing something uplifting, not something negative. We all know how draining the teacher who does nothing but complain about their students, parents, curriculum, lack of prep period, or air conditioning is.

Don't be the Negative Nelly that positive teachers try to avoid. Nobody ever complained their way into feeling better. I'm not saying the complaints aren't valid. Goodness knows teaching is fraught with challenges. But to focus on them exclusively is detrimental to our stress level and our health.

Practice Gratitude

Much has been written about the benefits of habitually thinking and writing down things we are grateful for.

Although there are many things to stress about in education right now, there are still so many things that we can be thankful for if we are intentional about looking for them and willing to dig deep.

For example, if you are reading this book, you probably still have your teaching job, a paycheck, and health insurance. You probably have a place to live, food to eat, internet access, a phone. If you are tired of all of your responsibilities and taking care of your family, realize how fortunate you are to have social connections and that you don't have to deal with loneliness. If you don't have the responsibilities of looking after your children or a family, appreciate that your free time is your own. You can read a book, you can choose what you eat or whether or not you want to cook.

During shelter in place, I was thankful that I had some flexibility with my schedule. I scheduled all my live video teaching in the afternoon so that I had the opportunity to get some exercise in the morning when I had more energy. I had the flexibility to quietly prepare my lesson plans at night, so I didn't feel guilty about spending an hour in the sunshine in the morning. Having the opportunity to go for a bike ride on a "school day" felt very indulgent.

One coworker was grateful she didn't have to spend three hours a day commuting. I realized that for the first time all year, I could be more creative in the curriculum and projects I assigned. Occupational self-direction is one of the most significant contributors to job satisfaction. It was something that I had missed.

You may be aware of the benefits of keeping a gratitude journal. Writing in it once won't have a long-term effect. The magic happens when we develop a consistent habit.

Here are some routines I have developed around this.

Before I leave school, I write down the top three bright spots of my day in my Positive Mindset Journal. This originated from a ritual I had with my children when they were young. Every night as I tucked them in bed, we would list the three favorite parts of our day. Even though my daughter is now an adult living away from home, sometimes at night I still get a text from her asking, "Three things?" It's a lovely mood-boosting habit.

Taking the time to share things for which you are thankful is also valuable. When you share your appreciation, you amplify it. Not only does the person receiving the thanks feel good, but sharing also extends the release of your happy hormones. So it's helpful to take time out every day to find someone to thank. An email, a phone call, or best of all, a handwritten note are all easy ways to thank people. Students, parents, coworkers, bus drivers, instructional aides, custodians, secretaries, administrators, coaches …there are literally hundreds of people at our school site that we can thank every day.

I like to select at least three students a week to "champion" and show appreciation for, with either a phone call or email home. It's such an easy thing and doesn't take long to do and yet it can make a huge difference in a student's life. Do you remember your teacher ever calling home just to tell your parents who much they enjoyed having you in class or how proud they were of your efforts?

During distance learning, I found I appreciated so many small things that I had taken for granted in the classroom even more when they happened during our daily Zoom calls. I was grateful every time we laughed or had fun together. Every time a student sent me a message saying something like *"Seeing you every day makes me feel better,"* or a parent thanked me, I had a heightened sense of appreciation for all of these things.

I also made an extra effort to reach out at least once a day to thank someone via email, such as a curriculum coach or a member of our tech department. They were still plugging along, working hard without the benefit of the "good stuff" and connection with students.

If you don't already have a habit of intentionally practicing gratitude, it is one of the easiest ways to boost your mood. There is a link at the beginning of this book to download a free six-week PDF version of The Positive Mindset Journal for Teachers. It is an excellent place to help you start tracking the three best parts of your day, and who to champion for the week. Enjoy!

Recognize All Things Change and Are Finite

At the time of writing this book, we are waiting on science. Waiting for a vaccine, waiting for immunity testing, waiting for enough people to recover from the Covid- 19 Coronavirus to have reached the "herd immunity" threshold. Maybe by the time you read this, all of these issues will be in the past. But based on the ease and frequency of international travel, it's likely this will not be our last pandemic crisis.

It helps to remember that all things are finite. The reality of providing teaching remotely or physical distancing in schools is not sustainable in the long run unless we reimagine entirely the way we deliver instruction. The teaching landscape is continuously changing.

I used to get stressed every time we adopted a new curriculum, a new "focus" for the year (usually with all the accompanying acronyms), a new set of teaching principles. At a certain point, I had to learn to take it all in my stride. When I was the lead teacher in 3rd grade with just one partner, that partner changed four times in three years. One of the partners was the district's former superintendent who was fired by the school board and then, mid-year, was back in a classroom teaching 3rd grade for the first time. Pretty crazy!

If we are in education for the long haul, it's best to remember that things are constantly changing. I generally look at changes positively, embracing opportunities for growth. But if something is moving in a direction I really don't like, I remind myself that it's one more passing show. It will eventually change.

Embrace the Opportunity to Rethink Education

Our shelter in place experience taught us that school is more than a building. Students rely on school for social and emotional needs, connection, and in a lot of cases, even food. School is a place that parents know their child can be safe for six hours a day while they go off to work.

It also brought into sharp focus the gross inequities in opportunities and learning experiences. Some students had access to their own devices and fast internet speeds. They could navigate assignments and participate in synchronous video chats and lessons. Others were at home with a packet of information and some without even the necessary supplies with which to complete them. The focus of their day was how to get to campus for their "grab and go" lunch and breakfast for the next day. Some students with school-provided devices needed to go to their local library parking lot to have access to free wi-fi.

The digital divide is real, and distance learning magnified the size of that gap. Hopefully, this issue that educators have been complaining about for years will now be in sharper focus and will become a priority for law and policymakers to address.

This can be an exciting time in education. We have the opportunity to change it for the better. While the world has dramatically changed in the last century, the method by which we have traditionally delivered instruction has remained relatively stagnant. We can take advantage of this shift that was forced upon us to reimagine our education system. We can upgrade our archaic system with something more dynamic and more appropriate to equip our students with the skills they will need in a more globally-minded economy.

Many businesses realize the advantages of having office workers spend at least part of their week telecommuting. I live in the Bay Area of San Francisco. Numerous tech companies are giving employees the option of working from home permanently, even when the need for social distancing is over.

Our students, the workers of the future, will need a new set of skills. Many of these skills, such as being organized, effectively managing their time and workload, and learning to solve problems and collaborate with others virtually, were skills we started to develop in distance learning. Moving forward, understanding how to leverage technology to share ideas will be a more relevant skill than memorizing state capitals.

We don't focus enough in the structured school setting on stimulating students' executive function skills such as self-regulation, setting priorities, and organizing tasks. The old school paradigm has needed to evolve, and this is our opportunity to make those changes.

My sincere hope is that we can use this opportunity to rethink the way we do things, and not just put on masks and "get through this phase" until we return to "business as usual." The mindset needs to be of redesigning and improving, not merely treading water until we get back to the traditional ways of doing things.

Define Your Teaching North Star

One of the recurring themes in this book is "less."

When I discuss the curriculum, it will be a matter of quality over quantity. We need to assign less.

When I discuss minimizing teacher overwhelm, the focus will again be on less. Doing less. Committing to less. Prioritizing self-care and recognizing when the work we do is "good enough."

In this section on mindset, I want to introduce the idea of "less" in terms of tuning out the external static thrown at us and focusing on our "teaching truths". These are the things we know to be true about what students need in order to learn, and what teachers need in order to be fulfilled and to support that learning. I call these teaching guiding principles my teaching North Star.

In retrospect, one of the things that contributed to my confidence in teaching unraveling was the fact that I stopped focusing on my teaching North Star. I was overwhelmed with new curriculum, new technologies, constant updates to instructional practices, many strong and diverse opinions about how things should be done, and a completely foreign school culture.

I had come from a school population of predominantly low and socially economically disadvantaged students. Many families were in crisis, and an overwhelming number of students struggled academically and emotionally. Much of my day was spent managing behavior problems, and I was heavily invested in trauma-informed teaching. It was tough, but I truly loved the school and the students. While it wouldn't be the preferred environment for many teachers, it was what I was used to and I was comfortable there.

My new school could not be more different. The majority of the students were academically proficient, self- motivated, and well behaved. The giddiness of this new reality, where I could focus on delivering high-quality instruction versus managing behavior all day, led me to assume that I could jump straight to focusing on moving students up Bloom's Taxonomy of Skills. I assumed I didn't need to worry about Maslow's Hierarchy of Needs. I assumed incorrectly. Just because students weren't coming from chaotic homes or suffering food insecurity, it didn't mean that they could learn before their needs for safety, love, belonging, and self-esteem were met.

I had been very distracted by details and was over complicating things. I focused on data and results without investing time in genuinely connecting with my students and fulfilling their basic needs for security and community. Once I returned to the foundations of my teaching compass, my fundamental truths, the energy in the classroom changed. We all began to thrive.

More details on these concepts will be discussed in the Classroom Management section of the book. But for now, here are my teaching truths.

Note, these are not areas written in a School Mission Statement anywhere. They are not posted above my desk. They are not concepts that I would repeat to an administrator in an interview if they asked me to describe my teaching philosophy. I am not presenting a teaching manifesto or telling people what should be relevant to them.

These are *my* truths.

These are the things that, in my experience and in my heart, I know to be important and they serve as my North Star. They keep me on track when I start to lose my way.

TRUTHS *About What Students Need to Feel From Me To Learn*

1. I see you.

2. You matter.

3. You are safe here.

4. I believe you can achieve at a high level.

5. Your success is important to me.

Truths About Teaching

1. Connection over curriculum.

2. Your energy speaks louder than your words.

3. Teach only love.

I encourage you to reflect on your teaching truths. If you are newer to teaching, please don't cheat yourself by thinking you haven't figured them out yet. Most teachers instinctively know what students need. There is an exercise in the Workbook to help you.

NOW THAT WE have looked at productive mindsets for thriving in our new teaching reality, let's move on to the specifics of how to set up our classrooms and curriculum for success.

2

Back to School Reboot

FOR THE FIRST ten years of teaching every summer I would re-read Harry and Rosemary Wong's excellent book The First Day of School, How to Be an Effective Teacher. It was a dog-eared copy, full of sticky notes and highlights. Towards the end of a decade, I could skip through it in less than an hour. Published in 1991, the book has become a staple resource for new and veteran teachers alike. But the teaching world has changed, and we need to reinvent what back to school looks like.

The main ideas of Wong's book are as relevant as ever. They center around investing time in setting up expectations, procedures, and routines in the first days of school to set the tone for the rest of the year. Along with the advice to set up rules and practice routines repeatedly before jumping in to the curriculum, the Wongs also lay out the critical elements of exhibiting positive expectations for all students and designing lessons for student mastery. To the best of my knowledge, the book is responsible for the "noun, verb, product" format of the measurable learning objectives that many of us have been required to write as part of our regular teaching routine. It's a classic, and veteran teachers have their back to school routine down to a well-rehearsed science.

However, knowing that we may need to pivot to online learning at any time, our new back to school plan needs to be updated to ensure we set ourselves up for success.

At the time of this writing, it seems that most schools will reopen in the fall in some form. The guidelines from the CDC observing schools in other countries that reopened before us suggest that students will be in class on a limited basis. A combination of staggered schedules (AM/PM or alternating days or weeks) and distance learning will be employed for at least a few months. Some states are also floating the idea that parents who do not feel safe sending their children back to campus may elect to have them participate in distance learning 100% of the time. It is unclear who will be providing that distance learning if teachers are in class teaching students on campus. Schools are also facing crippling budget cuts, so hiring additional teachers seems out of the question.

Right now, the plans are very dynamic. The situation is causing anxiety for parents and teachers, neither of whom have been consulted on how exactly this could work practically.

I am assuming that by the time you read this, a gameplan for your school will be in place. What has been decided may be beyond our control. But we can be strategic about setting ourselves up for success. Even if we have found a miraculous cure for this virus and school campuses are back to "business as usual" with all students in classrooms, a rapid retreat into distance learning will always be possible. We scrambled with our first worldwide shelter in place drill. Now it is time to reflect on best practices and be strategic about moving forward.

Specific details will change with our circumstances. But every plan should encompass the following elements.

1. Establishing rules and routines and practicing them repeatedly
2. Setting up a comprehensive communication plan with parents

3. Having an emergency distance learning plan ready to deploy
4. Critical skills to teach the first weeks of school
5. Building a classroom community

Let's examine each of these elements more closely.

Establishing Rules and Routines and Practice Them Repeatedly

During my years of mentoring, I have witnessed numerous teachers, keen to dive into "ice breaker" activities and new curriculum, skimp on the time they invested in this step. They all lived to regret it. I use the word "investing" correctly. Spending numerous hours for weeks at the beginning of school, repeatedly practicing routines can seem tedious and time-intensive. But it's a question of "pay me now, or pay me later." It's easier to invest time in doing it correctly at the beginning of the year than to waste time every single lesson, every day reteaching and reminding students of what they should be doing and how they should be doing it. Think of things your students do daily, such as lining up and entering a room correctly. Sure it takes an extra 5 - 10 minutes a day to practice. But after two weeks, the routine (and the fact that you are consistent in enforcing it) will now be a habit. It might need revisiting the first day back after an extended break, but that's still easier than the frustration and missed time of fighting that same battle every day for the180 days of school.

In the section on Classroom Management, I will do a deep dive into rules versus standards. But whichever you choose, at the beginning of the year, it is important to determine what they will be. It is critical to get student input as to what it looks like when everyone is following the rules. Teachers are more successful at this if they can somehow make it fun. Again, more on that later. For now, I assume you are familiar with the rules in your room and how you go about communicating them.

This year, the challenging area will be the new guidelines for physical distancing recommended by the CDC. Younger students will need a lot of practicing and reinforcement to stay distanced, appropriately ensure mask safety, and practice optimal hygiene around shared touch points. The routines will be new to both students and teachers, and no doubt we will learn through trial and error.

It will be more important than ever to be patient, as this will be stressful for everyone. Students whose parents may have strong opinions one way or another on these issues may be resistant. Staff, many of whom are in a higher risk category, may be concerned for their own safety.

Again, assume the best intentions. No one truly knows another's personal situation. People you assume to have low-risk factors may have loved ones in their household that they are afraid of infecting. Try not to make judgments if you feel people are being too cautious or not careful enough. Your school will have a series of protocols that it is your job to follow and enforce regardless of whether you agree with them.

Hopefully, schools will provide grade appropriate resources to educate students on the reason and importance of the new procedures. It will be especially hard for younger students with lower impulse control to understand and remember to stay distanced from friends and not go running up to their teacher when they want something. Until the new reality becomes routine, we must be prepared to invest more time than ever before in practicing procedures. Not just because it will make teaching more manageable in the long run, but because everyone's safety depends on it. These are high stakes experiments we are engaging in.

Setting Up a Comprehensive Communication Plan with Parents

I learned long ago from Steven Covey's amazing Seven Habits of Highly Effective People that relationships are like bank accounts - you need to make deposits before making withdrawals. For this reason, for many years, I have made it a habit to reach out to parents by phone as soon as I get my class list to establish a relationship. No one wants the first time they hear from their child's teacher to be when there is a problem, or when they are asking for something.

Teaching lower elementary, I have never had more than 30 students in my class. Calling all the parents has been a realistic goal, even in the years when some of them had dual custody arrangements, and I needed to communicate with two sets of parents. I understand if you teach a single subject, it will be unrealistic to try and call more than 100 parents, so an introductory email will have to suffice.

I keep my introductory phone call very brief. I let parents know how glad I am to have their child in my class, how committed I am to every child in my class succeeding, and to personally invite them to come to Back to School Night to learn all about our plans for the year. It sets the tone that I am not calling to engage in a long conversation, and I reassure them that all of their questions will be answered at Back to School Night. If I make six or seven phone calls in half an hour, and I can knock them all out in the first week.

Again, it's an investment of time and a substantial deposit into the parent's emotional bank account. It also allows me to figure out immediately if I don't have the best phone number for a parent rather than waiting until it is mission-critical that I connect with them.

During Back to School Night, I will be making it a priority to set everyone up for success. Recognize that for the 2020/2021 school year it seems that we will have to do Back to School Night in shifts to avoid excessive numbers of parents in the room. It will be inconvenient, but it will be doable. These will be the main areas I plan to address:

The logistics of what our everyday class routines for safety will be. Parents can have their concerns addressed and understand what their responsibilities are. If we return to a hybrid instructional schedule where students are involved in both in-class and at-home learning, then I will be communicating our Distance Learning Plan. I will talk about this more in the next section, but for now, recognize that it will be best to have one document that lays out the whole plan with a consistent daily or weekly schedule for parents. Ideally, make a one-page cheat sheet so that parents can keep it easily visible wherever their student will be doing their daily work. The easier and clearer we make it for parents, the more successful we will be.

Completing a home technology inventory. Even though I come from a privileged place of having one to one Chromebooks in my classroom that I can send home with students if I need to, I still want to know what everyone's situation is regarding internet access. This way, I can be proactive about providing parents with resources before it becomes critical. Also, many households have more than one student in them. I would like to get a good understanding of whom will need to coordinate the sharing of devices with siblings who also need to do schoolwork and homework.

Getting all parents set up on my preferred personal communication application. There are few places that you are teaching right now in the western world where parents are showing up to Back to School Night without a mobile/cell phone. In the next chapter, I will be discussing the use of apps that communicate directly with the parent's cell phone. I use Class Dojo and find it more effective than email communication for many reasons that I will go into later. But whichever parent communication app you choose (Remind, Class Dojo, Bloomz, Class Tag are just a few), it is helpful to set parents up on it right when they are in the room with you. Usually, it's just a matter of downloading the app and putting in a class code. Doing it together in the classroom will save a lot of time and questions later.

Completing a parent communication inventory. So many times, the information that we have for parents in our school database is incorrect. I have no idea why, especially at the beginning of the school year, when parents have probably just completed 10 pages of enrollment and emergency contact data. But it is still a fact that a lot of time is wasted tracking parents down, sending emails that don't get read, and contacting phone numbers that are no longer in service or have full voicemails. You already know all this. I always have parents fill out a simple form at Back to School Night with their cell phone number and one email address for someone in the household that gets checked EVERY DAY. I also ask their preferred mode of communication. I'm not always able to accommodate it, but asking gives them extra incentive to complete the short form.

Finally, I would cover much of the usual Back to School information that time allowed for. Class expectations, behavior plan, and consequences. In past years I have gone over restorative justice procedures, but that will depend on your class or school. I give a brief overview of the curriculum and standards. I provide specific information on how to communicate with me and when to expect a response. Managing parent expectations in this area is essential, and I explore it more in the Overcoming Teacher Overwhelm section of the book. In past years I would also discuss field trips and ways that parents could volunteer in the classroom, but I fear those areas might be obsolete for a while.

Questions from Teachers:

What about the parents who cannot come to Back to School Night?

Usually, I present my information on a brief slideshow. With all the new tech skills I learned during shelter in place, I now know how easy it is to add voice to that slideshow and put it on my private Youtube channel and email parents the link. I could also have someone just video me making my presentation and do the same thing. Either way, there is no excuse for parents not to have access to the information covered at Back to School Night. I plan on sending the inventories home or attaching digital copies to an email. I would follow up with a phone call to ensure that the information has been returned and set the parent up on Class Dojo, or whatever I'm using. Does all of this take time? Sure it does. But to me, it's an upfront investment that makes the rest of my year go smoothly.

What if students do not come back to campus?

I think the worst-case scenario for many of us is to start the year with no direct contact with the students. If this is the case, I would start with my phone call and invite the parent to participate in a mandatory video call to cover the same information. I would be sure to record the group video call so that it would be available for any parent who couldn't participate at that time.

I know that some schools do not allow live video conferencing. That's a tough one. I would suggest making an informational video, putting it on a private Youtube channel, and emailing the parents the link. Also, as far as recording goes, I would work with an opt-out scenario versus an opt-in, or you will spend way too much time tracking down permission slips. What I mean by that is if people don't want to be recorded they need to let you know, as opposed to you getting their permission. I use Zoom, and people can mute themselves and turn off their cameras, so no one should really have a problem with it. If they have a question and don't want to be seen or heard, they can send you a private message in the chat box.

What if you are reading this book in the middle of the year?

This is the same answer I give to teachers about changing their classroom management plan. You don't have to wait until the beginning of the next school year to make changes to your program! You can easily send home the technology inventory and communication preference forms at any time. Likewise, with setting up parents on your communication app. Each app has a printout letter with a class code to send home, or a "sign up" text sent to the parent's mobile/cell phone. However, there's no need to call parents in for a group meeting if it is not the beginning of the year.

Have an Emergency Distance Learning Plan Ready to Deploy

Teachers should have at least a few days of emergency lesson plans somewhere in their classrooms. Most districts require a minimum of two days. Whether you create them, borrow them, or buy them, it doesn't matter. Just so long as somewhere in the room, there are some "grab and go" activities and lesson plans that a substitute could use to keep your class moving smoothly in the event of a true illness or emergency were you unable to write lesson plans. They shouldn't introduce new material, but be engaging enough to keep everyone on task and feel successful in learning.

Just like we have physical emergency lesson plans, it will be helpful to have some engaging digital lesson plans and projects ready to go in the event of another emergency shelter in place. In the next chapter, we will explore the concept of "digital assets." It's enough to go through the best of what you taught during distance teaching and put it into an easily accessible format. Find a project or unit that is already done and put it aside for a digital rainy day.

For example, I have a whole set of read aloud videos complete with reflection prompts that I made for The One and Only Ivan. The students loved it! In the initial phase of distance learning when we naively thought we were only going to miss eight days of school, I was reluctant to press on with the core curriculum. I curated a selection of science videos, virtual field trips, readings, art, and writing activities around the theme of the solar system. During our daily Zoom calls, we shared our writing and what we had learned and even did some direct drawing of space-themed doodles. We had a lot of fun!

The activities were initially spread over the eight days, but I spent time this summer putting them into a week-long project broken into five daily slideshows. Both of these resources are ready to be deployed if needs be to buy me at least a week to set up a cohesive distance learning program and do appropriate lesson planning if ever needed. Neither of these activities is mandatory to be covered, so towards the end of the year, if I haven't needed to use them, I can assign them independently during class time as "fillers" while assessing students one on one. They certainly won't go to waste!

Critical Skills to Teach the First Weeks of School

Traditionally the first weeks of school have been used to review the previous year's learning, get a baseline measure of students' skills, and dive into the new grade-level curriculum. While it is going to be critical to administer assessments and gauge students' skill levels, I think there are other priorities before diving straight into pure content-based instruction. The prime concern should be on ensuring that students have the skills they will need to be successful when working independently in the classroom or at home. They can learn about the four geographic regions of California later, that's pure content knowledge. First priorities should be the following:

1. Ensuring everyone knows how to use the technology, applications, and websites commonly used in class and in distance learning. Regardless of whichever management system your district supports (Google C-Suite, Canvas, or Microsoft Teams, for example), make sure that you and your students know how to use the fundamental elements and practice using them. Do we know how to post assignments, see when they were turned in, give feedback, and grade them? Do students know how and where to find their assignments and how to turn them in? Spending time in class practicing these things will save you so much time and frustration later.

Find ways to use technology to help with community building and having fun. Practice, practice, practice. In the next section, I will make suggestions of what a distance learning plan could look like. But even if you are 100% classroom-based, I suggest making at least a few hours' worth of distance plans where students practice clicking on links, going to external websites to read and answer questions, watching videos, and taking formative assessments. If they have questions, it will be so much easier to answer them and show them when they are with you rather than trying to explain via email, phone, or having to screencast a video to show them.

Early primary grade students should also practice using the appropriate technology and apps. Even if they can't create documents, they are digital natives, they have been interacting with technology long before they started school. Many schools use programs such as Seesaw where younger students can take videos and photos to make a digital portfolio of their work. Have students practice using these tools sooner rather than later, even if it is tempting to wait until they are a little more mature later in the year.

2. Creating a password cheat sheet for each student and making sure they take a copy home.

3. Assigning at least one digital homework assignment so that any issues students have accessing technology and the internet can be discovered before it's a critical issue. Make it something very engaging such as a digital scavenger hunt or digital escape room exercise. Assigning some high-interest projects will help proactively troubleshoot problems as students find out logging in and turning in assignments at home can be different than logging in at school.

4. Teaching students appropriate research skills and how to evaluate the validity of the information they find. Our students have grown up in a world where "google" is a verb. Their default research strategy is simply to pull up a browser and pop in some keywords. Students need to be taught how to use the internet correctly, how to fact check, how to dig deeper than just citing the first piece of information they find.

In 2019, Stanford University researchers evaluated over 3,400 high school students' ability to judge the credibility of digital information. Two-thirds of students couldn't differentiate between news stories and ads that were clearly labeled as "sponsored content." The majority of students were also unable to recognize bias. 96% of them didn't consider that the credibility of a climate change website might be influenced by its ties to a fossil fuel company.

So it's essential to start teaching these skills at an early age. For younger grades, many teachers begin by exposing students to safe search engines such as Kiddle. The standard first research project is usually an animal report, where students can select something of interest. Students are introduced to kid-sized versions of reputable websites such as NatGeoKids.com or WikiKids.com.

These are all good first steps, but even younger students need to be taught that not everything they find on the internet is true. When teaching students as early as first grade, I have directed students to a website I own and had them look at the information. Then I would go in, change the information to something outrageous, and insert a picture of someone famous they knew and claim it was me. Then I would have them pull up the website again. They were amazed that I just changed something "on the internet". The website is actually a ".org" which many students feel is more credible. It is a powerful lesson.

I even suggest showing students something like GoDaddy.com where they can see how easy it is to buy a domain name. For fun, they can see if the domain name for their own name is already taken.

Remember the incident that led me to retreat to the supply closet and sob at the beginning of the book? It was shutting down a student who had a question I didn't have time to answer. Here's how I solved that problem. I set up a fun bulletin board in class titled "Curiosity Parking Lot." I attached a stack of papers next to it. If students had a question that they were curious about, they could write it on a slip of paper and attach it to the bulletin board. Whenever we had a few extra minutes, I would grab one, and students would research the answer.

This solved two problems. First, students felt they could get their questions answered, and I was able to model research skills appropriately. Taking a question out of the parking lot became a preferred "may do" activity for early finishers.

Mid-grade and older students definitely should be taught to be discerning about digital research. commonsense.org points out,

"Most of all, it's up to us to show students how to be skeptical of what they see on the web without becoming cynical."

Older students should be taught how to use fact-checking sites and engage in lessons where they evaluate web sources for bias. One of the best resources I have ever found on teaching students how to correctly "google" and truly understand points of view and primary sources is the 2016 TED Talk by Alan November, What is the Value of a Teacher?

In the talk November, a prominent educational consultant, contends teachers overestimate how much critical thinking students use when searching for information. If you are unfamiliar with the talk, I highly recommend listening to his account of working with a student who wrote a report on the Iranian Hostage Crisis. Ask yourself if your students would do anything other than what this student did, which was type in "Iranian Hostage Crisis" into google and go with the information presented, which is all from the Western perspective. Would you know how to teach a student how to effectively research the issue from the Iranian perspective and apply critical thinking to the problem?

If I taught upper grades, I would definitely watch the appropriate section TED Talk with my students and see how far they could get with the assignment. The whole talk is only 18 minutes. If you are not reading this on a digital reader with the link, just google "Alan November TED Talk, 2016." That part isn't tricky!

Also, for older students, teach them how to "show their work" for web searches with a simple graphic organizer. Media literacy skills are only going to increase in importance moving forward, and they need to be explicitly taught.

5. Discussing the responsibility and best practices of digital citizenship.

Most schools invest time in citizenship, character, and anti-bullying education of one type or another. Digital citizenship is a whole other issue. It is important to spend time at the beginning of the year setting expectations for both internet safety (password and privacy protection, phishing emails, pop-ups that can cause viruses, etc.) and internet etiquette.

Cyberbullying is a big problem. It happens outside of the classroom, with even younger students having their own phones and iPads. The issue is further complicated when the school issues the device and requires it to be used off-campus in the case of distance learning.

While every district has a technology policy that students and parents must sign, we all know how stressful it is to be perceived as responsible for managing things over which we have no control. Here's an example. During shelter in place, my third-grade students had their own "google hangouts" and sent messages to each other.

They did this on their own, outside of any requirements I had for collaboration.

Clearly, I have no control over what they choose to do on their own time in their own home, even if it is on a device the school provided. One morning, I received an email from a parent saying that their child hadn't slept all night and was extremely scared because another student had sent her a chain letter in an email.

I remember chain letters from my childhood when, old school style, we got them in the mail. They usually contain a scary story and a threat of a curse if you don't forward it to ten other people—that kind of thing. The parent sent me the email. Let's just say it was graphically violent and disturbing. I spent the whole day playing detective, trying to figure out who had sent it to who, calling parents and students, and my IT department.

Students were scared first by the content, and then some of them were afraid of telling their parents because they had lied and said they were doing required school work when they were on hangouts with their friends. I emailed all parents and reminded them that if students make their own chat rooms, there is no supervision provided by the school. In addition, I had specific Zoom calls with the entire class about the issue. The IT department confirmed that the letter did not originate in my class.

Nonetheless, parents' perception was that it was something I needed to resolve and manage. Don't get me wrong; they were my students, and they were scared, so I felt absolutely motivated to help. But are these things a teacher's responsibility? The lines are very gray here. Time, energy, and resources were wasted. Worse, students were scared and stressed. In extreme cases, cyberbullying is a factor in teen suicides.

It is easier to see how the teacher can influence this when we have students with us six hours a day, it's less obvious when working with them remotely. The answer is to invest time upfront in digital citizenship lessons. If your school has not already adopted resources for this, I urge you to invest adequate time in finding your own. I understand there are so many things to cover at the beginning of the year and it's tempting to rush through these lessons. But having students role-play and really understand the power of their words is such an important skill. Everyone is becoming increasingly reliant on sound bites, tweets, quick texts, and emojis to communicate. Students who have grown up spending a lot of time chatting via a screen need to be explicitly taught that feelings are real, not just graphics.

If your school does not have an adopted curriculum, plenty of free digital citizenship resources are available through the Common Sense Media website at commonsense.org.

Building Class Community When on Campus

If you have been teaching for a while, you probably have a repertoire of tried and true "ice breaker" type activities for the first week of school. These are activities where students get to share things about themselves and learn about their classmates. The activities vary by grade level, and Pinterest and teacher forums have hundreds of them if you are looking for some new ideas. These activities are fun and engaging, but community building in a classroom needs to go deeper than learning about a classmate's favorite food, movie, book, or video game.

In my school district, we have an excellent professional development process called "Walking and Talking." Teams of teachers and administrators visit classrooms of varying grades on campuses different than their own. They observe instructional practices and student engagement and reflect on what they see. Talking with and observing teachers and administrators with whom we have no working relationship facilitates reflective conversation without the fear of being judged and is very effective for professional growth. Classrooms are observed and rated on six areas. The first area to be evaluated is the classroom "vibe." To score the highest level on vibe the following needs to be observed:

"The tone of the lesson and the general atmosphere of the classroom is student-friendly and has a high degree of positive energy, with a focus on actively engaged students learning and high levels of student outcomes."

That's a pretty tall order and every teacher's goal. Having high expectations for all students, everybody working together to achieve them, supporting each other, feeling safe to take risks and grow, and positively demonstrating learning doesn't happen by accident. It takes a skilled teacher, and it takes intentionally cultivating class community. So how do we accomplish this, especially with the reality that we may be living within the constraints of "physical distancing" and having our students come to school in shifts?

First, involve the students in setting up the class standards or rules. Center the discussion about what type of classroom environment and "vibe" they want to experience. Again, there will be more specifics in the Classroom Management section. Obviously, you want to steer the conversation in the direction of "everyone feels respected," "everyone supports each other's learning." Define synergy and explain how working together everyone can learn more. When setting up your class rules, standards, and procedures have fun role-playing and practicing. It's not productive to simply post on the wall, "Show respect." Invest time in modeling and discussing, "What does showing respect look like?" and "What does it sound like?"

Next, foster the notion that the classroom is everyone's home. Let's face it, in the traditional school day, we all spend more time in the classroom than in our living room. For lower grades, I make sure the student's photos are on the wall, along with at least one piece of art or writing that the students have done. You can display the "ice breakers" from the first days of school. Here are some grade-specific examples:

About Me Bag. Lower-grade students can take home a brown lunch bag and fill it with no more than five things that represent them.

They take five minutes in class to present and can choose questions from three students to answer. This helps with learning names! Students love pulling things out that are important to them. If five students a day present, it takes no more than forty minutes a day for the first week to go through the entire class. This exercise also provides an excellent opportunity to model and practice respectful listening. I like to take a photo with the student and their objects and put it up on the wall.

About Me T-Shirt. It's fun for slightly older students to complete a template of a blank t-shirt on a piece of paper. Students decorate the t-shirt with things that are important to them or draw pictures for sentence prompts such as "My favorite...." Again, students take turns sharing with the class. I take a photo of the student and put it on the page somewhere and display it on the wall. This project can be modified for upper grade students who can incorporate graphic design concepts to digitally create a t-shirt logo that represents them. Again, display them on the wall.

Another thing I do to foster the idea that the room is everyone's space is to have students vote on certain aspects. One entire wall of our room last year was a huge computer monitor. Whenever I wasn't using it to present, I would have a moving screen saver with tranquil ambient music. Youtube has many ad-free ones. For example, in winter, I would have a huge crackling fireplace. Other favorites were jellyfish, aquariums, the galaxies, nature scenes. I would set it up before the students came in, and they would be excited to see what the theme of the day was. Often they got to vote on it. I loved it when students had looked for some at home and came in all excited to share it. I like to take advantage of any time I include an element of shared choice in the classroom's physical look or vibe so that students take more ownership of it.

The best type of community building that happens, of course, is organic and not as a result of preset "activities." But these take time.

It amazes me for 18 years, even though I have been teaching in the same room with essentially the same elements of curriculum, every group of students has been unique. Every year there is something unexpected that totally engages them and captures their imagination.

One year I had a class who was really interested in the rain forest. One year a class was fascinated with slime. Another class was really excited about the day we spent at the Pioneer School and historical school artifacts. Each year, I try to find one project that we complete together that is not to do with academics or the curriculum directly. We work together as a class, and, to be honest, at the beginning of the year, I have no idea what it will be, but one always emerges.

For example, for the class that was crazy about all things rainforest, we organized a coin drive to donate towards deforestation. From making posters to counting coins, students loved it. I still proudly display a certificate that says the class saved 70 acres of the rain forest. The slime class and I made every conceivable sort of slime, including glitter and magnetic slime. Students researched recipes and brought in supplies. For the class that was fascinated with artifacts, we did a time capsule project and had a burial ceremony with the custodian. That was quite a few years ago. He and I have since left the school, and I'm smiling now, wondering who will eventually discover it.

Anyway, you get my point. Each class has its own personality. Getting involved in a project together that has nothing to do with the day to day curriculum is excellent for community building.

If older students have something they are passionate about, they can develop an assembly or video presentation to share with the rest of the school. The opportunities are endless.

Hopefully, you will have an entire year with your class to find their personality. But it's still important to invest the time at the beginning of the year to engineer opportunities for community building, even if it feels less authentic.

Fostering a "teamwork" culture will be a little trickier if we need to enforce physical distancing. Some of the traditional classroom ways of doing this will need to be modified if students aren't able to sit in small groups or wander around to be peer helpers. I use a lot of small group instruction in my classroom, and students know when we're doing rotations that they should help others at their table or ask for help from at least three other students before seeking my help. You may know that as the "three before me" rule.

Needing to be separated in the classroom does not mean that students can no longer collaborate. They can do so digitally with shared documents, or maybe setting up desks in large triangular configurations. We need to be prepared for voices to be louder if students are further apart, but the models that school are looking at right now need to include fewer bodies in a room at any given time, so hopefully, that is a trade-off.

In any event, students at the beginning of the year need explicit instruction and reminders about how to work collaboratively. How do we assign roles to ensure that everyone's strengths are capitalized on? How do we give feedback that is meaningful and kind?

Regardless of age, I like to teach students how to give "glow and grow" feedback. That means that after a presentation or when giving feedback on a shared project, students need to find something positive to say and something that could be improved upon. Younger students will benefit from sentence frames such as,

GLOW

"My favorite part was when…"

"The thing I found most interesting or surprising was…"

"Something that you did that I really liked was…."

"I can see you worked hard on…"

GROW

"I would have liked to learn more about…"

"I think it would be interesting if you could add…"

"I had a hard time understanding…"

"I think maybe another/better choice might be…"

Don't always assume that older students are more practiced in giving constructive peer feedback. They might also benefit from specific modeling at the beginning of the year.

Shared visions and goals, getting to know each other, investment in the classroom space, effective teamwork, and community projects are all some ways that we build community when our students are with us on campus. But what about when they are not?

You may remember that one of my teaching North Stars is "Connection over Curriculum." In the next section I will explore building community and increasing student engagement while putting together remote learning curriculum.

Part II

CONNECTION, COMMUNITY, CONSEQUENCES, AND CURRICULUM

3

Connection Over Curriculum

WHEN I LEFT school on Friday, March 13th, 2020, I had no idea I would not be going back to my class until the end of the year. When I did, it was to sadly pack up my students' belongings. Surreal, to say the least. Maybe your situation was similar.

I was lucky to be in a pretty privileged position. All of my students had their own Chromebook in class. The following Monday, it was a mad scramble to disinfect devices, get them picked up "grab and go" style, and prepare to engage in distance learning. That's right! We had one day to prepare. Considering I had never even heard of Zoom or scheduled assignments on Google Classroom previously, I'm proud of how my class and I rallied. By that Wednesday, I had my own YouTube channel (ironic for the teacher who tells kids, "YouTuber is not a career").

Of course, a whole nation of teachers did precisely the same thing. Many of us while also juggling having our own children at home with us. It wasn't perfect, but it got done. We're teachers, we always find a way to get it done. We even pulled off drive-by celebrations because we missed our students and wanted to have fun with them.

We came up with creative ways to honor their rites of passage, such as graduations.

As of the time of writing this, most of those bags of students belongings and work that I spent 10 hours packing up are still sitting in our multi-purpose room like abandoned artifacts of a bygone era (*"Remember our Maker Space where students huddled together and touched the same components? What were we thinking?"*)

Anyway, I'm not sure what your experience looked like, but based on all the memes I've seen on social media, I can assume it was pretty similar. Students quickly figured out that our state had a "hold harmless" clause, which meant teachers could only be given a "credit" or "no credit" grade on their year-end report card. While some students thrived with the types of projects I assigned, I think it's fair to say that most of my students were not living up to their learning potential. I sure was! I learned so much during our distance learning "trial by fire." Here are my biggest takeaways.

1. Less is more
2. Connection over curriculum
3. Students still need a choice and a voice
4. Don't use new tools to do "old" work

Truthfully, I already knew these things, but our shelter in place experience confirmed their importance.

It's still unclear if we will be providing distance learning in the upcoming fall, but now we all live with the reality that teaching remotely will always be a possibility. On the bright side, many of the new skills I learned will undoubtedly be applicable and relevant to in-class instruction. If we are 100% on campus, it seems that next year I will be teaching a combination class of two grades. The challenge with that in the past has always been how to keep one grade on task while I am giving direct instruction to the other. The apparent answer now would be to set up the same resources that were used for distance learning for students to work on independently (or collaboratively) while they are actually in the same room with me.

I'm thankful that I was pushed a little out of my comfort zone to learn how to best leverage educational technology.

Avoid using a $1000 pencil

In his TED Talk, Alan November cautioned against using technology as a "$1000 pencil". By that, he means don't get seduced into using expensive technology just to do the same tasks we used to do with paper and pencil.

Examples of this would be scanning pages of your textbook into PDFs and posting them on Google classroom for your students to read. Or spending hours converting your regular worksheets into Google slides with the text boxes where students can type in the answer. There are better ways to use technology.

Most current textbooks have digital versions where students can interact with a text by highlighting and annotating. Instead of creating five grammar sheets for your students to complete, generating a minimum of 100 slides of student work that we need to correct and give feedback on, we could invest time in locating software that will differentiate instruction and provide immediate feedback. The time we save converting PDF's and grading, we can more productively spend on evaluating the data the software collects and conferencing with students to remediate specific skill gaps.

I am committed to "walking my talk" and not giving an overwhelming number of software or computer application suggestions. If your school has already invested in one to one student devices, I am guessing they already have accounts set up for you with many of these programs. I know that was certainly true for me. We have the tools, I just hadn't invested enough time to learn them all. When tasked with producing emergency distance lesson plans, many of us defaulted to what we and our students were most comfortable with. Now is the time to prioritize ensuring we are all comfortable with the best programs.

If your school does not already have a preferred set of programs they support, I courage you to do some research on your own, reach out to other teacher ed-tech groups, and make some recommendations. edweb.net/onlinelearning/ has a plethora of resources if your district does not have a technology department or you are unsure where to start. Even without district support, you can make free accounts for your students on such sites as Freckle, Readworks, MobyMax, and Khan Academy Mappers. However, be sure to check the account requirements for each program against your district's student data privacy policy to ensure compliance.

Less is more

One common theme in this book is that "less is more." In this section, I will talk about the need to assign less. In the section on classroom management, I will discuss why we need to talk less. And in the section on reducing teacher overwhelm, I will give specific feedback on how we can excel as educators, even when doing less.

One mistake I made with my first digital lesson plans was to try and emulate the instructional path of a regular day in the classroom. For the sake of trying to keep things as "normal" as possible, I curated lesson plans that covered math, language arts, a read aloud, a science or social studies lesson, a daily Zoom call, and office hours. I even provided art, music, and PE lessons on the same days that we experience in the classroom. It was a good example of "using a $1000 pencil" and putting my students and me on the fast track to burnout and exhaustion within a week. Trying to provide six hours of daily instruction because that is what we were used to in class was unrealistic and counterproductive.

If you have done any work in your school around Professional Learning Communities (PLCs), you may be aware of the 2003 research by Robert Marzano. He calculated that the content standards teachers are expected to address would need 22 years of instructional time to be adequately covered. The calculation was based on 13 hours of class time during the K-12 school system, equating to over 5 1/2 hours of direct instruction a day. Although I have no official data, I do have 18 years of experience as a teacher and 13 years of experience as a student to back me up when I say I think even 22 years is a gross underestimation.

Consider this. If we subtract lunch break, recesses, PE, passing periods, transition and cleaning up, the time we spend giving and repeating instructions, dealing with classroom management disruptions as well as school interruptions such as assemblies, drills, announcements, school spirit days and early release days, is the number of hours a day students actually spend learning anywhere close to five and a half? Not even close. So when curating resources and lesson planning focus on high-quality assignments that make the best use of technology, have the highest measurable student outcomes, and allow students to acquire true 21st-century skills. That is a tall order for lesson plans, but less is more. Far better to assign three hours of quality work a day, than six hours of busy work.

I recommend working with a backward design mentality. If you have done any work with PLCs, you know that the first order of business is to identify the essential standards that students need to master in your grade. If you have not already done this with your team, it is a great place to start. I still remember the day I realized it was my job to teach the content standards, not just the textbook exactly as it was. Many of the essential standards were towards the end of the book, and due to an early end of year testing schedule, I was forced to rush through them. Work with your grade level or subject matter teams to differentiate between what are the "must-have standards" and "nice to have standards" and work backward from there to ensure the most important content matter is all covered.

Even if your school does not work with the PLC model, you can use their 4 Guided Questions to plan the most meaningful learning assignments for your students. They are:

1. What do we want students to learn? **(essential standards)**

2. How will we know if they have learned it? **(team-developed common assessments)**
3. What will we do if they don't learn it? **(systematic interventions)**
4. What will we do if they already know it? **(extended learning)**

DuFour, R., DuFour, R., Eaker, R., & Many, T. (2010). Learning by Doing: A Handbook for Professional Learning Communities at Work Bloomington, IN: Solution Tree Press

Remember that less is more, both with assignments that are synchronous (live participation) and asynchronous (worked on when a student chooses to). I found that students were much more apt to participate in our live video meetings if they were no more than once a day, and only 30 minutes in duration unless we worked in breakout groups. Of course, students always had the option to come early or stay on if they wanted specific help with something. Attention spans are even shorter online when students have instant access to snacks, TV, video games, pets, or even their siblings if they are babysitting. It's a lot easier to minimize distractions in a classroom, so shorter online sessions were more effective.

Basic Components of a Digital Learning Plan

Here are some necessary components of a distance learning program. I encourage you to go with the "less is more" theory when deciding which applications and programs to use. There are literally hundreds of resources to support teachers and students in distance learning. No doubt, your email inbox has been flooded with suggestions from well-meaning technology departments, curriculum coaches, and colleagues. We don't need 100 resources! We just need four or five good ones that our students are comfortable with and meet our basic needs :

1. Providing both synchronous and asynchronous learning

2. Offering opportunities for collaboration and community building
3. Allowing for assessment and the collection of grades and data and sharing feedback.

At minimum, a program would need these four basic components:

Learning Management System (LMS)

An LMS is the "hub" from where all assignments and communications are launched, and grades are collected and archived. If your school is a G-suite for Education School, this would be Google classroom. Other popular platforms are Canvas, Microsoft Teams, and Moodle.

Video Conferencing Platform

2020 was definitely the year when "Zooming" became a commonly used verb, even outside of education. The two most popular platforms for teachers to interact with their students in real-time were Zoom and Google Meet. Both are easy to use, and both have advantages and constraints.

A Video Recording Software

Many free options are available. I set up my own YouTube channel and used YouTube Live to record my morning messages, lessons, and a daily read aloud. I set the channel settings to private so that only students with the links had access to the videos. Screencastify is a Chrome Browser extension that is very easy to use and allows you to record your screen, as you narrate.

An Interactive Sharing Program

Students will need some way to explain their thinking, collaborate, and give each other feedback. An easy way to do this is to use a program such as Seesaw for lower elementary students and Flipgrid or Padlet which is a virtual bulletin board for older students. These programs allow a teacher to post content or questions and for students to post video feedback responses of their thinking process and work.

So that's four basic elements. In addition, you would have all the usual websites and programs that students regularly use for writing, reading, science and social studies content and for quizzes and assessment. But the goal is to organize and deploy all of these different elements through the LMS.

Here's an example of what my lesson plans looked like, I think it was relatively standard for elementary and middle school. Our school uses Google classroom. I organized my Google classroom into topics, each topic being a week.

Although I provided daily lesson plans, everything other than math was due on Fridays. This was to give students flexibility if they were sharing devices at home or had limited access to Wi-Fi. It also provided flexibility for students who needed help from their parents who were still working and for students who had the responsibilities of looking after their siblings. Some projects I assigned lasted more than one week, but having all the assignments listed as one topic a week, was the easiest way to help students and parents stay organized.

My daily lesson plans were in the form of a Google slideshow. Everything that students needed to read, watch, or write was all embedded in the one slideshow as "one-stop shopping."

The first slide of the day was a video of my morning message and the second slide was always the information for our daily Zoom call. For math, I would embed a video of direct instruction that I had made or found online (thanks Khan Academy and Engage New York!) and then a link to an external site where students completed the skill's independent practice. No need to reinvent the wheel, many websites such as Assistments and Edulastic have pre-made independent practice and exit tickets aligned to most common curriculum and push the results directly back to the Google Classroom grade book. I would mix up days when the students selected an answer and when they needed to screen capture, showing their work and their thinking.

Part of the problem with distance learning, especially when working with a high achieving population, is that you are never quite sure of the validity of any scores. I'm sure many of you suspected that certain students had their parents or older siblings "heavily involved" in their work. I had a few students who struggled in class mysteriously score 100% on assessments. On one Zoom call, the whole class witnessed a mom completing the real-time quiz questions for her child before realizing we could see her and turn off their camera. Sigh. This was one of the reasons for our daily Zoom. Part of it was for social-emotional learning and connection, and part was for me to check for understanding on the day's math assignments and do any reteaching that needed to happen.

The rest of the slides pertained to the other content areas with links to appropriate videos, readings, and projects they were working on. To minimize the number of assignments turned in daily, I would make a copy of the slideshow for each student and insert blank slides where they answered questions, wrote their reflections, and did short writing assignments. They would "turn in" the whole slideshow. This way, I only had one assignment per student per day to grade and give feedback on.

Friday had little new work and was the "catch up" and math quiz day so that I could diagnose any reteaching of skills that I would need to do the following week. It was also Zoom Fun Day (more on that later).

None of this is revolutionary. But it is just one example of how to simplify workflow. In addition to the daily class Zoom, I also had a morning and afternoon "office hour" where I was available online for any student to email, Zoom, call or text me for help with anything they needed.

One of the best time investments I made was to create short screencast videos of how to do everyday tasks such as turn in assignments, navigate getting access to the student's school book marks on a home computer, etc. I set up a "Common Questions Resources" section on the Google Classroom page, and more than half of the parent and student inquiries I received could just be referred straight over to the videos.

Divide and conquer! Decide with your teammates which areas generate the most questions and divvy up, making short explanation videos. If you don't have a tech-savvy team or a team at all, just Google "How to _____ for students" (example, "how to turn in Google Classroom assignments") into Youtube and some kind teacher will have already made the resource for you. You can simply place the link on a "Resources" section of your LMS. Be sure to "enable" the video to be viewed by your district server as many school servers block random Youtube videos.

If you have older students, you can even assign the task to them. I am embarrassed to say that when we started distance learning, my students didn't know how to turn in digital assignments via Google Classroom because in class, they just emailed them to me. On my end, I could only see the teacher's view of the interface. On our first class Zoom, I had one of the students grab his older sibling who I knew used Google Classroom in 7th grade daily. The student "screen shared" on Zoom and showed everyone how to do it. In retrospect I should have asked him to make me a video, I'm sure he would have been happy to do so.

Developing a Communication Plan

Whatever format you decide for your distance learning program, I recommend that you keep it as consistent as possible. Provide a specific plan to communicate what your program will look like and define specific roles and responsibilities for students and parents. Here are some areas to make sure you address in your communication plan.

For Asynchronous Learning:

- Where and when will the teacher post assignments?

- When will assignments be due?
- How will students turn in assignments?
- What is the procedure if a student has a question about an assignment?
- How should students expect to receive feedback on their assignments?

For Synchronous/Live Session Learning:

- Will all students be required to attend?
- What is the process for informing the teacher if they cannot?
- What are the rules and behavior expectations for participation and live sessions? (for example, are students required to have their cameras on and their voices muted unless they have a question?)
- How will absent students check in with you?
- Will you be recording all sessions for students to access if they are unable to attend live?

For General Communication:

- What will your daily/weekly office hours be?
- What is a reasonable timeline for parents and students to expect a response from you to the emails and messages?
- How often will you communicate grades and or missing assignments to parents?
- How will students be expected to collaborate and communicate outside of live learning sessions and breakout rooms?
- What is your policy for facilitating these sessions?
- Will parents need to be advised that these interactions will not be moderated by a teacher?

Cultivating Connection When Distance Learning

In the previous chapter, I explored how to foster a classroom community when students are in the room with you. If you are providing blended learning, then it will be relatively easy to prioritize using those strategies to create community when students are in the room with you. It will be a little trickier to connect with students you have never met, but it can be done.

I recommend having students participate in some sort of icebreaker activity, just like they would in class. Students could post short videos answering "All About Me" prompts on Seesaw or FlipGrid. Be sure to put a time limit on the videos! Older students are probably familiar with a discussion board format. For them, you might set up a forum where they can share introductory Tik-Toks or whatever short video format is the current rage. Allowing them to express creativity in a fun way right at the start of the year will help with the perception that they will enjoy the class and be more engaged.

Unless you have a large cohort of students, make it a priority to video conference with every student one on one during the first week of school, or with the parent and the student if they are younger. This will be a considerable time investment, but it will pay off in the long run. This will be a time to get to know your students and have them learn about you, as well as a time to help you proactively troubleshoot any technical issues. It will also be an excellent opportunity to help students set up a study plan that works for their particular situation.

Providing a "one size fits all" study plan is not really feasible when every student's home situation varies. Taking the time to learn about your students' responsibilities and routines outside of school will help you connect with them and set them up for success. Some students will need specific guidance on how to manage their time and workflow and even their workspace. We need to be mindful of equity and access even if we know the student has access to a school-provided device. Not all students have a quiet place to work, they may need to share their equipment with siblings, and they may have responsibilities that make it difficult for them to show up on a daily live learning session. We need to be understanding and flexible.

To find time to conduct these conferences, I recommend that for the first few weeks of school, you assign high interest, fun projects for students to participate in that need minimal involvement (or grading) from you. Just like in the classroom, the focus for the first few weeks should be on practicing the technology and routines and getting to know each other.

If you teach a single subject or high school and have too many students to make individual conferences feasible, you could conduct live video calls for small groups. Be sure to host more open office hours the first week to help students individually who need assistance organizing their study plan.

Have Fun

One of the most authentic ways for students to build community is to have fun together, even if just virtually. When in the classroom, Fridays have traditionally been the day for my students to take quizzes and assessments, catch-up on assignments and projects, and have fun in the afternoon. With distance learning, I kept to the same schedule. I assigned a formative math assessment but no new work. Most projects were due on Friday, so this gave students a chance to catch up and make sure they were starting the next week fresh. It was also my day to catch up on grading, record videos and plan for the following week. However, I kept a daily Zoom appointment, and we had a class Zoom Fun Friday. Students got to vote on what they wanted to do that Friday.

Here are some suggestions:

Scavenger Hunt. Have students run around the house collecting objects to display on video before a one-minute timer goes off. This is great fun for younger students who love to be active and running around the house, giggling, and enlisting family members to help.

Show and Tell Pet Day. Students of all ages enjoy showing off their pets. The well-behaved ones become regulars mascots in our daily calls.

Spirit Days. Set up a fun theme for the day, such as crazy hair day, superhero day. You know the drill. During shelter in place, students were exceptionally resourceful and creative as they couldn't leave the house to buy supplies.

Direct Draw or Art Lessons. I'm not much of an artist, but there are plenty of short, direct draw videos on YouTube for all ages and interests. Simply run the video while you share your screen and complete the drawing along with the students. Then everyone shares their work!

Talent Shows. Students can showcase their talents live on a Zoom call or record them on Flip Grid or SeeSaw or something for you to compile beforehand. The latter method takes a little more preparation, but ensures that nothing inappropriate or too long or too boring happens during a live video meeting.

Bitmoji/Avatar Day. Challenge students to make their own Bitmojis or avatars and use them for their static screen ID photo. Once you all know a little bit about each other, it is fun to have students change their name on the screen to conceal their identity and have everyone guess which avatar belongs to each student.

Interactive Quiz Games. If you teach students how to split their screen, it is easy for them to play online quizzes like Kahoot during your live video conferences. You can develop your own content-rich quizzes as an additional check for understanding of the week's topics or select some pre-made quizzes that other teachers have created and shared on the site.

Incentives. Whenever possible, I would try and give out incentives on Friday. For example, the top three students to win a Kahoot were excused one day worth of assignments the following week, excluding multi-day projects, of course. On the Fridays when we were not playing a game, I would put a ticket in a hat for the students who had participated in every live video conference that week. Two students will be randomly selected to receive the assignment pass. Not surprisingly, I usually had 90 - 100% participation in my Friday Fun Zooms. It helped build class community and relieve stress before the weekend. Video conferencing fatigue is real, and by the end of the week I certainly needed something high energy and a little less structured to keep me motivated. The students probably felt the same way.

Again, let the students vote on what they want to do on Fun Fridays. Ask them for suggestions. Remember, whenever possible, give students a choice and a voice.

Teaching remotely, it may seem that the opportunity to just relax and "hang out" with kids to build connection is no longer an option, but that is not true. You could still hold a "meet with the teacher" lunch once a week via live video conferencing. The stipulation would be no talking about assignments grades or schoolwork. The meeting agenda would simply be social to connect and learn more about each other.

Jason Fried is the author of the book REWORK and the founder of a company that develops productivity tools for working remotely. He builds community in his company by hosting monthly "5-12" meetings. Once a month, he selects five random employees who only ever work together virtually. They have a social interaction video conference to get to know each other with the same rule - no work talk. Teachers can set up the same randomized schedule for a weekly or bi-weekly "social hour" (or 30 minutes) between students. As you are setting this meeting up, I recommend that you monitor it, even if you have your camera off and your microphone off. This way, you could continue to do work, but students would be aware of your presence and should be less prone to discuss anything inappropriate.

Here are some more points about moderating and supervising live video conferencing. My suggestion is that teachers moderate any interactions they set up. Older students may end up collaborating on their own via Google hangouts by sharing documents and obviously, teachers cannot moderate all of that, although we can routinely remind students of the responsibilities with regards to digital citizenship. I like to use the Zoom breakout room function for students to collaborate together during certain times. When I set that up, I am sure to rotate between the rooms every few minutes to facilitate discussions, check for understanding, and ensure the students are on task and appropriate.

Many schools have policies that prohibit teachers from being alone in a room with a student. For this reason, I suggest recording any one on one sessions that you have with a student, just to protect yourself. Let parents know that they are welcome and encouraged to be present in any one on one meeting with their children. Reassure the parents that the videos will not be publicly accessible or shared with anyone other than by parental request. Check with your school policy for best practices regarding this.

Mental Health/Social-Emotional Learning

With so much curriculum to cover, it can be hard to find time to meet students' social and emotional needs. Students need to feel safe in their online learning environment to make mistakes without being judged, to persevere, problem-solve, and to take risks with their learning.

Be sure to spend time exploring the concepts of growth mindset, and to provide ample but structured opportunity for students to reflect on their feelings and share them. Once a week I would put a short motivational or "character counts" type video in the lesson plans along with a morning message. Students could write a video reflection that they shared only with me.

If your school does not have an adopted program or resources, you can find a wealth of information at these two sites.

https://www.commonsense.org/education/toolkit/social-emotional-learning

Lessons and resources on Integrity and Self-Control, Humility and Gratitude, Curiosity, Empathy and Compassion, Courage and Perseverance, Teamwork and Communication

https://www.pbis.org/ Positive Behavior Intervention Support

My students knew I would start my daily Zooms ten minutes early for any student who wanted to just "talk" about issues before without the rest of the class (I enabled the waiting room and just admitted students one at a time).

One of our many unspoken responsibilities as an educator is to model emotional wellness. I like to start the first few minutes of our daily live meeting, engaging students in a "mood check." Sometimes to get the conversation rolling, I play music as students enter and see if they can guess my mood based on the tempo. Sometimes a quick visual poll and check-in (thumbs up, down, or sideways) — anything to facilitate the conversation that our feelings are valid and quickly discuss ways to feel better. I would send any student who seemed particularly out of sorts a private message to stay behind after the meeting was over for a few minutes.

While it is not our job to play school counselor, be mindful that students have limited access to trusted adults outside their home in a distance learning environment. We need to be sensitive to this and provide support where we can. We still have responsibilities as mandated reporters of child abuse and neglect, and we must continue to be attentive to students who are in vulnerable home situations.

Assignments that Foster Choice

I like to think of the assignments and projects that I created during distance learning as digital assets. While they may take longer to put together in the beginning, they are assets that can easily be tweaked and deployed again in the future.

For example, think about specific videos you record for asynchronous learning of a particular content area or standard. In theory, it should take you less time to record than it would to present it in front of the class as you will not be interrupted and have to manage behavior. It will take time to load it up to a server and to develop a system to keep your videos organized. However, once recorded, it is a digital asset that you can use again and again in future years. It can also be an excellent resource for any student who misses on-campus instruction. They will have the opportunity to watch you teach the lesson virtually in class on their device or at home.

Early on in our pivot to distance learning, my students mentioned that one of the things they most missed about being in the classroom was having me read to them. I read some shorter books on the daily Zoom calls, but the students wanted to listen to a novel. I let them vote on which book I would read, and then I broke it down into 15-minutes segments. I recorded the segments on YouTube Live. It takes a really long time to upload a 15-minute video, but YouTube Live saves them with no wait time. I set the privacy settings on the videos to only be visible to people I share the link so as not to violate copyright laws. Each day in my lesson plans, I would post a 15 minute read aloud along with a slide where students would write structured responses and reflections.

The students chose The One and Only Ivan, a story based on a real gorilla who had lived in a cage in a mall for 27 years before being relocated to a zoo. I developed a unit around the book, including longer writing assignments in the opinion, expository, and narrative genres. As Ivan was a real gorilla, I also assigned a research project about him, and students had a choice of how they presented the information they found. I curated science resources around gorillas and their habitats etc. This is now a "grab and go" digital asset that I can deploy if we ever need to make a rapid pivot back in to distance learning again. I can also use it in class next year, especially if I teach two grades simultaneously. One group of students can listen on their devices with headphones while I read a different read aloud to the other students.

When creating longer assignments and projects as digital assets, I am mindful to run them through these four filters:

- Can I add an element of choice to this assignment?

- Can I add an element of collaboration to this assignment?
- Am I using the best use of technology or a $1,000 pencil?
- How can I minimize my involvement in this project?

It stands to reason that students will be more invested in assignments in which they have an element of choice. This also makes for a more diverse spectrum of projects, therefore, increased opportunities for students to learn new skills and perspectives.

Giving students an element of choice can be accomplished in a few ways. First, they can choose the subject matter of a given assignment. For example, state reports, biography reports, endangered animals, ancient civilization reports are all standard assignments where students can choose what they want to learn and present about.

Next, we can incorporate some choice into the mode students choose to demonstrate learning. Allowing students to present their learning via slideshows, videos, infographics, podcasts, song lyrics or short skits instead of defaulting to written documents and quizzes will not only keep students engaged and encourage collaboration, but minimize the amount of reading and correcting reports that teachers need to do.

Certainly, younger students will need more structured support such as sentence frames in a slideshow, but older students are digital natives, and they are more likely to need help with organizational skills and time management more than how to use the technology. Not all assignments will be conducive to incorporating an element of choice, but we should try to include it whenever possible.

Be open to student ideas about technology that we may not be familiar with. I read a great lesson plan for an ancient civilizations unit where students created digital simulations of ancient cities using Minecraft EDU. Minecraft EDU can be used for math, history, science and coding assignments. Their site is full of ideas and engaging lesson plans. Remember,

choice = ownership + increased engagement

The easiest way to integrate choice into lesson plans for younger students is to assign a choice board. Assigning a board at the beginning of the week and giving instructions on how many "choices" need to be turned in by Friday is also an easy way to give families flexibility in when work can be completed. Clearly, daily math and reading lessons are "must dos", but choice boards work really well for "may dos" and additional practice.

Older students can have more flexibility in designing their own passion projects. Although they will need less help with technology and daily Zoom check-ins, they still need structured support. Providing them with rubrics and timelines and checking in at least once a week for a progress update is important.

It's a great idea for teachers to model the design and workflow by choosing their own project to complete alongside their students and sharing their thought processes and progress. As more companies adopt "work from home" options as part of their regular routine, learning to manage productivity and deadlines with minimal support will be an increasingly crucial 21st-century skill. Distance and project-based learning provide a natural opportunity to help students cultivate these.

Assignments That Foster Collaboration

Another foundational skill for 21st-century workplaces is virtual collaboration. Increasingly in office and tech environments, people work in teams that often spread across the globe. The office and tech workers of the future may rarely meet their colleagues face-to-face, and yet they will need to have productive working relationships. As an example, I have never met the cover designer, typesetter, or even some of the editors of this book. The cover designer lives in France, I outsourced promotional graphics to someone in India, and one of my editors lives on Taiwan. This is the world of global commerce that our students will graduate into.

For students who are used to communicating via text, Tweets, emojis, and soundbites, conversational competence is becoming a dying art. For these reasons, it is critical to incorporate opportunities for collaboration in our digital lesson plans. It's one thing to have "turn and talk" partners in class and work in small groups. It's entirely different to facilitate a discussion on live video conferencing with more than 4 or 5 students present.

One solution is to use digital breakout rooms. Most video conferencing applications allow you to assign smaller groups into breakout rooms to hold virtual discussions. The teacher can circulate the breakout rooms and bring everybody back together into one session for group sharing and debriefing.

Remember that younger students will need more structure and support when working in groups, including assigning clear roles and responsibilities. They also benefit from sentence frames for giving feedback. Older students can capitalize on each other's strengths. When assigning groups for projects, work with a combination of letting students select their own group members, and having you assign heterogeneous group members.

Students need to learn to work with others of varying skill levels and different personalities. If they always choose their own groups, they are likely to stick with their friends or the high achieving students they know will do most of the work for them. Let's be honest, in the real world we often have to work with people we would prefer not to. It's helpful to start developing the communication skills and stamina required for this in school.

Older students will coordinate their own video chats for collaboration. Routinely send them a reminder of digital citizenship best practices and etiquette.

Aside from synchronous teamwork, collaboration can be built into asynchronous assignments. Document sharing between small groups of students where they can comment on, add information and edits on written documents and slideshows are an easy way for students to collaborate. They can share research and ideas on digital bulletin boards such as Padlet.

One way to expose students to real-world learning experiences and collaboration is to video conference with experts (such as real time virtual field trips) or even with other students around the world. When I was in school, learning French was mandatory. We practiced our language skills by adopting penpals from France. We were so excited to write and receive those letters! There are many resources to match up classes around the globe, not just for penpals but, if it works with different time zones, live video conferencing. A quick google search will give you more resources than you can follow up on. My favorite is PenPalSchools, which was created by teachers to facilitate global project-based learning. It matches classrooms across the globe by grade level and topic interest, and students collaborate on projects. If you are interested in finding out more information, you can go to https://www.penpalschools.com/

Some Quick Tips for Minimizing Your Workflow

For those of us who had our classroom routine and curriculum down to a science, this may seem like an overwhelming amount of new skills to learn and work to be done. We all know the difference between the teacher who has taught for 30 years, and the teacher who has taught the same year 30 times. Let's not be the latter! We live in a dynamic world and, as educators, we need to rise to the challenge of giving our students new world skills. Our days of pulling the "October" tote off our shelf and taking out all the tried and true activities and lesson plans are gone. But that doesn't mean that we need to do all of the work ourselves.

I'm not advising taking shortcuts that will negatively impact student learning. However, I am advocating being strategic about managing our workflow. As I mentioned earlier, "vibe" is important. If a teacher is exhausted, always behind on their grading, and spending 12 hours a day in front of the laptop, the vibe is going to be that teaching and learning is an overwhelming chore for both the teacher and the students. None of us do our most creative planning and problem-solving when we feel we are continually struggling to keep up with our responsibilities.

An extensive list of general strategies will be presented later in the minimizing teacher overwhelm section, but for now, here are some tips to help us minimize our workflow when providing distance learning.

Divide and Conquer If you have three teammates and four content areas to plan, take one each, and then share your lesson plans. If you don't have a cohesive team or teach alone, go with the teacher mantra of "beg, borrow or steal." So many lesson plans are available online. Join some grade or content area specific forums or social media groups and share resources.

Don't Reinvent the Wheel There is no need to reinvent the wheel. Add to "beg, borrow, and steal" the word "buy." Some of the best "digital assets" I have created began as resources I bought from Teachers Pay Teachers for a few dollars and spent about an hour enhancing or tweaking to meet my needs perfectly. Spending a few dollars every couple of weeks to save hours of work is worth it to me.

Enlist student help Students love to help. Instead of coming up with additional "enrichment" work for students who complain they are bored (yes, I had that!) find ways for students to help. Students can look for or even develop content-rich Kahoots or similar type quizzes for the class to play. Older students can create "how-to" videos to place in the resources section of your LMS. This is especially beneficial when the student's view of an app or software differs from the teacher's view.

Have students peer edit whenever possible. Set up a buddy system for even younger students to check basic grammar or spelling pages for each other before they turn them in.

Avoid "Shiny New Technology" Syndrome One of the hardest skills to acquire in the digital learning space is what I call "tuning out the noise." Every day we are inundated with shiny new software, technologies, apps, and websites. Spending time on social media teaching sites can make us feel insecure. It can feel that others are being more creative and innovative than us.

I remember receiving an article that was titled "The 75 Best Technologies for Distance Learning." As I said before, my students and I don't need 75, we need four or five that we are familiar with and that deliver what we need. There's no value to continually changing the technology you use just for the sake of it. Evaluating and learning how to use new technology is a huge time investment. Once we're comfortable with it, we have to teach it to our students and support them through their growing pains. Unless tinkering with new technology is a passion of yours, I recommend being selective when committing to new apps, websites and computer programs.

"Tuning out the noise" means sticking with the basics that we know deliver for our students and us and not being distracted by what everyone else is doing. Of course, collaborating with our teammates and learning what is working for them will always be productive. No one knows your students as you do, and you are perfectly capable of diagnosing which technologies and types of assignments will work best for them.

Follow the 80/20 Rule There is a principle used in business, process management, and productivity known as Pareto's Principle. Named after an Italian economist, the principle states that 80 percent of outcomes are determined by just 20 % of the inputs. For example, in some retail areas, 80% of the sales come from 20% of the customers. In a school example, we might guess that 80% of the behavior problems come from just 20% of the students (I'd say less than 20% but who knows). You get the idea. In time management and productivity, the principle is that 80% of the results come from 20% of the work. Focusing on the basics will get us 80% there, the other 20% from "there to perfect" takes up a considerable amount of time with relatively little payback.

I am not suggesting that we put a 20% effort into our assignment planning or post sloppy work. But I am suggesting that not everything we need to do needs to be the best thing anyone has ever put together. Some days, "good enough" is going to be the best you can do. The time we invest in making something perfect could be better spent in other areas. Many of the digital assets I put together were good enough. Not all of them generated the best work for my students. I went back and put in the extra work to make the more productive assignments perfect so that they could be ready to go next time around.

Many teachers invest a lot of time in finding perfect graphics and fonts to make our assignments look beautiful. Themed graphics, while cute, don't affect student outcomes. Many students, given a choice, would take a cheerful, positive teacher over pleasant graphics. When budgeting your time, accept that two completed projects at 80% may provide more value overall than one perfect one.

Be strategic Don't feel guilty about finding shortcuts. For example, when assigning independent practice for math, I had two options for apps and websites. One needed to be scored by hand. The other scored the multiple-choice answers automatically and pushed the scores directly into my Google Classroom grade book. As the questions were essentially the same, the latter was clearly a smarter choice for me to use. Examine your procedures, and if streamlining doesn't negatively affect student learning, don't feel bad about doing so. There are lots of ways that technology can help us work smarter, not harder.

Now that we have explored how to leverage technology and digital assignments to be engaging and most impactful to student learning, it is time to answer the question, "How do we manage student behavior and minimize interruptions when students aren't in the classroom with us?"

In the next chapter, I will answer that question by doing a deep dive into the components of a comprehensive classroom management plan and how the same principles apply for digital and blended learning.

4

The Seven C's of Effective Classroom Management

FOR A LONG WHILE, I have been working on a book called <u>The Seven C's of Effective Classroom Management</u>. Unexpectedly, I had a family crisis that took up most of my free time for a year. Then a teaching crisis that stole my time and confidence. Two years passed without much writing happening. Then, just as if to mock me for proclaiming that bad things do *not* happen in threes, the Corona Crisis came a knocking on our global door. It became apparent that teachers needed support in other areas, beyond just classroom management.

However, classroom management is still one of the areas that causes teachers the most frustration, stress, and burnout. Just as important, if we don't have a handle on managing behavior, it gets in the way of students learning. So I am dedicating a large section of this book to help with this area.

For whatever reason, classroom management has always been a challenge I have enjoyed. I love the diversity of personalities, backgrounds, learning styles, and unique skills that children present. For me, being a teacher is like being a conductor of an orchestra. The challenge is to get everyone to harmoniously move in the same direction, each with their unique part to play and their own instrument. Synergy at its best. A symphony of learning! Well, most of the time.

I think being a parent before I was a teacher has been helpful. I spent quite a bit of time researching parenting styles when my children were young. Luckily, I stumbled on Parenting with Love and Logic by Jim Fay and Foster W. Cline. Although I haven't read the book in a long time, it introduced me to the ideas that have shaped my parenting and teaching. I also had plenty of trial and error with my own children.

After 24 years as a parent and 18 years in a classroom, this is what I know for sure about children:

Students need a voice, a choice, and the security of limits. Many students will take negative attention over no attention, so everyone's day will go smoother if you find a way to give them positive attention. Many students who are traumatized don't even know why they are acting out. Give them some grace, don't take their behavior personally, and diffuse the situation rather than engage.

I have worked with many populations of students from the most behavior challenged, traumatized, academically low, and underserved to the most privileged, self-motivated, and gifted. And the same holds true for all of them. If they are engaged and enjoy being in class, if they feel safe and respected, they will behave better regardless of their backgrounds.

Now, clearly, there are some outliers. I hate it when "experts" say, "If students are engaged in learning they behave" as if the only issue is a boring lesson and that the teacher is inadequate in some ways. I know amazing teachers who have had students in their class with such severe behaviors that they literally need a "room clear" emergency exit strategy to keep the rest of the class safe from the student when they have a "behavioral episode." No amount of "engaging content" is going to magically fix those issues. In fact, the more respected your classroom management skills are, the more likely it is that those students will be placed in your class. It can feel like some kind of back-handed compliment.

It is a growing burnout factor in schools that resources such as counselors and psychologists are being reduced while the number of students coming to us in crisis is increasing. Teachers are frustrated about not getting students the interventions and help they need. Often just one student's extreme behavior can hold the rest of the class hostage from learning and there is little teachers and administrators can realistically do about it. I have no solutions to that problem. But for 90% of your classroom management woes, the seven C's will definitely help.

So what are the seven Cs?

The first three were a gift given to me by a friend before I was a teacher. He and I were in the back seat of a car with my infant first child in the car seat between us. She was sleeping and angelic-looking, and we were both in awe of how smooth her little chubby thighs were. Although I was in my 30s, I had never spent any time around children. I had no younger siblings or cousins, and only one friend had a baby, and she was a new mom too. The friend in the car was completing his PhD in child psychology and was working as a family therapist. My daughter was already a few months old, and it occurred to me that most of my experiences with her thus far had been about caretaking, not really parenting. But that day would come.

As she slumbered peacefully and my usual state of high angst parental stress was temporarily calmed, I decided to hurriedly seek advice from the "expert". I asked him, "In ten words or less, give me your best parenting advice." It took him just three words. "Calm. Consistent. Consequences." I repeated those three words like a mantra at every Back to School Night for over a decade when explaining my classroom management plan.

As time went on and I reflected on my teaching practice, I realized that much of my success with classroom management could also be attributed to four more Cs - connection, collaboration, communication, and cheerfulness.

Let's start with my classroom management truths about students first. What do I mean when I say that children need a "voice and a choice"?

One of the most stressful classroom management situations is when a student engages in a power struggle with the teacher. No teacher ever wins an "argument" with a student. The only result is wasted time, frustration, and often the rest of the class losing respect for the teacher. So most teachers are experienced enough to know not to engage in an argument. We'll talk more about this later. But why are some students so confrontational to begin with?

Everyone has a basic human need to feel noticed and validated. Power struggles are an attempt for a student to control a situation when they may feel they have no control over so many other areas of their life. "A voice and a choice" refers to giving students as many opportunities as possible to feel noticed, important, and empowered. Allowing students to have agency in as many areas as possible will dramatically reduce power struggles.

Clearly, teachers are ultimately in charge, and not everything can have an element of choice to it. But we all know a power- crazy teacher when we meet one. They have rules just for the sake of rules and demand compliance. Their battle cry is, "Because I said so!"

Much of this is the same as the classroom vibe discussion. Remember my teaching truths? "I see you. You matter." It's the same idea. Validation is a strong human motivator. Giving students a voice and a choice will be a common theme in having a productive day in the classroom.

The next key idea to understand is that of setting limits. Children are curious. It's also part of their growth process to push boundaries and see how far they can go. Students need to feel safe to learn. A chaotic classroom without clear limits is very stressful for students. A classroom where limits are enforced some days, for some students, but not in other situations is even more so. Students don't know what to expect. Some children think they would love to be in a school with no rules. They wouldn't. Not because there would be violence and bullying and anarchy, but because it's stressful not to know how to act and what appropriate behavior looks like. Children are often acting out to test the limits, and understanding them aids in developing self-control. Limits say, "You are safe here."

OK, so let's look at the seven Cs.

CALM

I thought I would be the first parent to never yell at my kids. I was wrong. Shouting at a child, "It's not OK to raise your voice!" is as ridiculous as smacking a child because they hit someone. And yet, in class, we sometimes do it (the voice raising, not the hitting). The class is loud, so we talk louder and louder until we are almost shouting, "You guys, it's too loud in here!" If we could take a step back, we would see how counterproductive this is. But it's hard to take a step back when you are doing your teacher dance, juggling technology, instruction, interruptions, behavior issues, and well, being human.

Being a calm teacher goes beyond counting to ten when you start to get worked up. It's the ability to not get worked up in the first place. Calm is being quietly in control of your emotional reactivity. It stems from self-assurance and practice.

Here are several strategies will help you develop calm:

Perspective

Practicing the mindsets from the beginning of the book will, over time, help you maintain perspective. Not all of the students in your class are defying rules or challenging boundaries. Non-compliant behavior can indeed be disruptive and take away class time, but don't let it take up all your mental energy. If you allow your conversations with colleagues and friends to be only about the two students who are driving you crazy and you ignore the fact that twenty other students are cooperating and learning, you have lost perspective. Focusing all of your energy on minor annoyances while ignoring the broader picture is a damaging habit.

Confidence

I remember when I substituted middle school for the first time. I found the class very challenging. Most of the students were taller than me, and it seemed that they had extrasensory powers like dogs; they could smell my fear. I was insecure about my ability to control the class and they sensed it. I naively got goaded into a power struggle with a student who was being disrespectful.

I learned the hard way that engaging with a student is a no-win situation. The discussion will likely escalate, and if the teacher has to resort to giving a harsher consequence as a result, they can end up losing the respect of the class. After a few years, I had enough confidence in my classroom management skills that I simply expected things to go smoothly. If something didn't, I had the confidence that I could handle it calmly.

Confidence comes from experience and also from having an effective classroom management plan that we are comfortable with so that we don't feel that we have to come up with solutions on the fly.

Don't take things personally

Very little about what other people do is directly about us. Some students come to school angry and out of sorts. Many of them have plenty to feel mad about. Avoid buying into the narrative that a student is trying to challenge or upset us or ruin our day. Their behavior may be the result of many factors over which neither of us has control. That doesn't mean that we allow students to be disrespectful to us or others. It just means we don't take their behavior personally.

Focus on the behavior, not the child

"Where did we get the idea that we can get a child to behave better by feeling worse?"

Dr. Jane Nelson

This should be self-explanatory. Calmly state the rule that has been broken without berating the student. For example,

"Josh, the rule is not to disrupt the class. Your choice is to stop disrupting others or spend some time by yourself at the quiet table. Which do you choose?"

As opposed to,

"Josh! You are so disruptive! Go and sit at the quiet table. I'm tired of telling you the same thing every day!"

Demeaning a child, nagging, or worse, shaming by saying something like,

"Everybody is fed up with your attitude, Josh! You are eating everyone's time!"

is unproductive, hurtful, unprofessional, and an abuse of our power. We are the adults in the room, and as such, we need to model appropriate interactions.

Mindfulness exercises

One area that can help us develop more calmness in all areas of our life is to have some sort of mindfulness practice. Reactionary responses are automatic. We need to accept the idea that between a stimulus and our response, there is a brief moment of pause. In that pause, we can choose a different response. Mindfulness won't help us in the immediate moment; for example, if we are already engaging with a student, there is already too much negative momentum propelling us forward. Practices such as "brain breaks" or counting ten slow breaths help when we feel our energy and stress rising before an incident occurs.

One of the first things I teach my students is "starfish breathing" or "take 5 breathing". We all practice it together as a class when we need to settle our energy, such as after coming in from the playground when students are often rowdy and preoccupied with what social interactions they encountered on the yard. It is a simple conscious breathing technique to help children to learn to connect to their breath, calm down, and relax. It is suitable for students of any age, from kindergartners to seniors.

Once we have a real sense of community in class, I take it as a positive if students can sense I am getting irritated with someone or something, and one of them suggests, "Shall we do some starfish breathing, Mrs. S.?" While I might be disappointed in myself that I let my irritation show, I appreciate that I have taught my students a tool that they can use to self-regulate their emotions. It makes me happy to see students using the technique without my suggestion. Of course, the trick is to cultivate a class culture where no one would make fun of them or think any less of them for using it.

Starfish breathing is a straightforward technique. Like anything, it needs to be practiced until everyone is on board. I suggest having students practice it with their eyes open the first few times so that they can see everyone and realize that no one is "weird". Here's how to do it. Extend your left arm and open the fingers of your left hand. Place the index finger of your right hand at the wrist of your left hand. The idea is to slowly trace your index finger around your fingers, coordinating your breath, until you arrive at the wrist on the left side. As you move your fingers, inhale on the way up the finger and exhale out on the way down. It should take about 20 - 30 seconds.

If you find these instructions confusing, hop over to YouTube and type in "Starfish Breathing". It is a very common intervention, but don't be fooled by its simplicity! It can be very effective.

At the end of the Workbook you will find a bonus mini ebook on how to incorporate mindfulness in your everyday life.

Lower your voice

Although it sounds counter-intuitive, one of the easiest things you can do to keep your class volume at a manageable level is to lower your own voice. We've all taught next to the teacher we can hear through the walls. Don't be that teacher! If you are quieter and more intentional with your words, students will listen. Talk less and talk less loudly. Honestly, it's a game changer. Talking louder and louder as your class gets louder is just a bad habit. Like anything else, with practice and intention, it can be changed. Later I will talk about hand gestures, which will enable the teacher to manage a lot of behavior without talking at all.

CONSISTENT

You may remember learning about ineffective parenting styles in child development class. Obviously, strict authoritarian styles and totally permissive styles are both ineffective in the long run. But inconsistent and unpredictable parenting is equally, if not more, damaging. When children are unaware of the limits, and when consequences are randomly enforced, they become anxious and have attachment issues. Chaotic parenting, which alternates between bribes and being loving, then yelling and harsh punishments, leave children uncertain of the way rules of the world work and how to properly follow them.

It's the same with classroom management styles. Some teachers survive by being totally authoritarian. They are uncompromising; they have a reputation for instilling fear. They are generally unliked. It was decided long ago that blame, shame, and pain have no place in the classroom. Other teachers want to be "friends" with the students and have a reputation for being totally lenient. Their classrooms are often loud and chaotic and stressful for quiet, compliant students who want to get their work done.

The teachers who struggle the most are the inconsistent ones. They are stressed and overwhelmed. They repeat themselves, nag, try to negotiate with students to convince or bribe them to behave. When they finally get overly frustrated, they raise their voice and dish out random consequences. Classroom behavior is chaotic because students see the boundaries as flexible and try to push them.

For students who feel out of control in many areas of their life, pushing the teacher to frustration and the "yelling point" becomes a sport. Not because the student is being malicious, but because they feel they can control at least one outcome in their life with their behavior. It is hard not to take their behavior personally, but it often has to do with their circumstances and trauma, not you.

The key to an effective classroom management plan is consistency. If we have a rule, we need to enforce it calmly, confidently and respectfully every time, regardless of the student and irrespective of the circumstance. If our plan is students get one verbal warning, then a consequence, we need to be prepared to follow that every single time. If we don't, not only will students keep testing the boundaries, they will not feel safe in the classroom.

It also becomes a fairness issue. Students will start to think that we have different rules for different students and that some are preferred over others. That's very harmful not only to the self-esteem of the students who perceive themselves as being "picked on", but also to the classroom sense of community.

CONSEQUENCES

I tell students that just like in science, where every action has a reaction, in life, every choice has a consequence. Some of the consequences are good, some of them aren't. So when we talk about consequences, we should not only set up consequences for undesired behavior, but also for desired behavior. Consequences are feedback on how students are doing.

Consequences should be designed to help students learn from their choices and not intended as a punishment. To be most effective, they should be logical and related to the behavior so that learning can occur. Whenever possible, they should also be predetermined so that there are no "surprises" for students.

For example, if a student fails to follow playground equipment rules, the logical consequence is that they are unable to play with it for a time, not that they serve lunch detention. Depending on the age of the student and the severity of the infraction, the student might get a warning or reminder, but they should be made aware of what the consequences of their choices would be. Here's one example:

"The rule is feet first on the slide. If you break the rule again, you will not be able to use the slide for the rest of recess (or the week, if the student is a repeat offender). I trust you will make a good choice."

Here are some more:

Students take too long to log off their technology and pack it away when doing a preferred activity, so the next time they need to start "packing up" 5 minutes earlier (make sure it is during their preferred activity time).

Students intentionally make a mess in the cafeteria, so they need to stay in from lunch recess to clean it up.

A student is having trouble staying on task and is disrupting others at his table so they need to sit at a "quiet" desk for a while (a desk in isolation away from their friend zone).

These are all pretty obvious consequences.

We need to avoid doing what ineffective classroom managers do, and that is make repeated non-specific requests,

"You guys, settle down!"

Or criticize,

"Why can you guys never work quietly?"

This gives students no concise direction as to precisely what the desired behavior looks like.

Saying, *"Shhh!"* is not giving a specific instruction.

Typically frustration will build until a teacher dishes out some random threat such as,

"You are all going to lose recess!"

which the class knows the teacher doesn't even want to enforce. It's the equivalent of a parent yelling, "I'm going to cancel Christmas!" Everyone knows they are not going to follow through.

TOKEN ECONOMIES and PAT Time

Remember that there should be consequences for good behavior, too. Some teachers debate that handing out student rewards in a token type economy is "manipulating" student behavior and that the goal should be to have self-motivated learners.

I agree that ideally, students should do what is in the best interests of everyone learning and cooperating, and we want students to develop self-efficacy. But our classrooms are populated with students with attention differences, those with low impulse control, students who have no positive role models for respectful limit setting, and students who have a desperate need to be noticed and validated. If we only focus on poor behavior, we will quickly train those students to act out if they feel that is the only way to get attention.

I prefer to hand out individual rewards to students as opposed to table points. Table points can lead to resentment of students who are prone to losing points for the entire table.

For many years I passed out tickets as I circulated the room to recognize students on task or helping others. It was a way of giving feedback without having to talk.

Sometimes we would make it into a game where I would hand out tickets to the first three students who had their books open to the right place and were ready to learn, or at the end of the day just hold a strip of tickets in my hand and start circulating and handing them out to students who were cleaning up the room. You'd be surprised how quickly other students pitch in when they notice and how efficiently a room can be cleaned without me having to ask.

At the end of the week, the tickets went into a drawing where 5 or 6 students could choose from small prizes, a Buddy Pass (sit next to a friend for a day), Couch Pass (we had a luxurious couch where two students a week could sit and do all of their reading) and a Homework Pass. In lower grades, the "Line Leader" pass was always very coveted!

The "currency" that students care about will differ by grade. Upper-grade students typically liked to earn a "Music Pass" where they could listen to music on their phones for a period.

It is important to note that I never took tickets away from students for poor behavior choices. If they earned them fair and square, they got to participate. There have been a couple of students I would proactively look for on the yard before school or when lining up to "catch them doing something good" before they even got in the door. It seemed to make a big difference for them.

Even if you don't agree with token economies, there should always be a positive consequence that students are working towards. I like the idea of PAT time, as it is a logical consequence.

PAT time stands for "Preferred Activity Time." I learned about it in Robert MacKenzie's excellent book, Setting Limits in the Classroom. For many years I reserved an hour on Friday afternoon for PAT time. Any student who had completed their work for the week could have an hour to engage in preferred activities.

In lower grades, I had puzzles, manipulatives, Legos, magnets, and other games that we had no time to work with during the week. Older students usually opted for free time on technology working on non-educational sites. Coincidentally, I always work with a weekly homework packet that is due on Fridays. So if a student had unfinished work from the week or did not hand in homework, there was an automatic hour in the day on Friday for them to get caught up. Of course, they would miss their PAT time and get an opportunity to experience a real word consequence.

CONNECTION

"No serious learning can occur without a serious relationship."

James Comer, Professor of Child Psychology

The longer I teach, the more I am convinced that connection is one of the critical components of success in the classroom. If students genuinely feel that you have taken time to know them and understand them, they will feel seen and safe and ready to learn.

Connection happens as a result of time investment and authentic experiences.

While the "getting to know you" activities I talked about for the first days of school are important, they are not the source of genuine connection.

Every parent knows that "connecting with children" isn't as easy as reserving a time block on the weekly schedule like a family meeting. It occurs when spending relaxed downtime with students, and this is hard to achieve when every minute of the day is on a tight schedule of mandated instructional minutes. So we have to be creative about finding the time. I generally spend part of the day in small groups with students. Whenever we have a few extra minutes at my table, I engage in conversations that aren't focused on academics. If we are doing art, I sit next to some students and follow the art lesson with them.

One school I worked at served breakfast before school and the students knew that on Thursdays I would show up early, stand in line, give my lunch number and sit at a table with my yogurt parfait tray. A small group of students from my class would quickly assemble, and we'd just eat and chat. I set aside one day a week to eat lunch with students in my room. Students can drop their names in a container if they are interested in participating, and I randomly select a small number of students every week. If the students need to buy lunch from the cafeteria, we go together to collect them, bring them back to our room, or sit on the yard outside if the weather is nice. Being lucky enough to live close to my school, I make an effort to attend plays and concerts. If I had any athletic inclinations, I would choose to coach a sport as one of my adjunct duties.

If all of these areas are going to be impacted by the temporary need for physical distancing, I'll have to get more creative. But connecting with students will be an even higher priority if they are suffering the effects of an extended shelter in place isolation.

I feel any time that I can spend with students outside of delivering curriculum or feedback is a valuable investment. Not because it pays off with better behavior, but because it's easier to like people when we understand them. And I want to genuinely like and enjoy my students.

One important caveat is that a teacher's interest has to be genuine. Just like the fear radar, students also have a pretty good instinct for when adults are being fake. When a student seems out of sorts first thing in the morning, and you quietly take them aside to ask them if anything is going on that you can help them with, they know if you are genuinely interested in helping or just playing lip service to your role as a mandated reporter.

It's challenging to come up with specific steps for "connecting with students". Either teachers are genuinely interested in getting to know and understand people they are going to be spending a whole year with, or they are not. Clearly, it's easier to connect to students if we are in a self-contained classroom with fewer students for the entire day than if we are serving up to 150 students a day in 45-minute increments.

One way to increase the opportunity for connection is to allow the students to get to know you better. Share appropriate personal stories. Use humor if you are funny. Let your personality shine through.

COLLABORATION

There are two areas of collaboration that are helpful to reflect on. One is collaborating with peers, the other is collaborating with students.

While on campus, it is helpful for teachers to have a "discipline buddy". This is a colleague's room where you can send a student with work if the two of you need a break from each other. Once in a while, it happens. It is better to send the student to a colleague's room where they can be supervised and encouraged to stay on task than to the office if you just need to spend some time away from each other. Obviously, extreme behavior and defiance earn students a direct trip to the office. But here I am referring more to a quiet "time out" than a discipline issue.

When selecting a discipline buddy you should select a colleague with whom you have an excellent working relationship, similar teaching styles, and who is a friend you can count on to help you out without judgment. Ideally, it should be a reciprocal arrangement. A discipline buddy is also handy when it comes to PAT time. Students from both classes who have earned free choice activities can stay in one classroom with one of the teachers, and students who need to complete work can remain in another classroom with the other.

On a side note, only send students to the office as a last resort. For some students, leaving the room is a reward. And unfortunately, frequently sending students to the office reflects poorly on the teacher. I know that doesn't seem fair when some of us end up with a disproportionate amount of behavior problems in our room, but administrators often have short memories of their time in the classroom. The teacher who frequently needs an administrator's assistance with behavior issues can be perceived as having weak classroom management skills or a lack of patience or compassion for troubled students.

While I discourage the bad habit of complaining about students, everyone needs at least one colleague who can be a "safe place" to vent and share some humor about all the craziness students bring to our day. If we can't find one on campus, we may need to look outside to find our crew. It's essential to have people we trust to listen to us without judgment, even if they are not teachers.

Collaboration with students can come in numerous forms. First, I suggest you work with your students to come up with class standards and rules together. This way, they have some buy-in and ownership of how the classroom runs.

If you have a healthy class culture of collaboration, there will be far fewer interruptions to teaching and behavior issues. Students will naturally start helping each other when appropriate and encouraging their classmates to stay on task.

Restorative Justice

In the last few years, many schools have adopted a Restorative Justice approach to managing students' conflicts and discipline issues. This system empowers students to work with their peers in small groups to gain understanding and air grievances. Students are encouraged to reflect on how their words and actions have affected others. Needless to say, this involves collaboration and teacher involvement at the beginning to model moderating and positive communication.

If a consequence is assigned by an administrator, the goal is to move away from automatic detentions and suspensions and assign a project that has learning and an element of restoration to it. For example, if a student has been bullying another, they might be assigned a research project on the long-term effects of bullying and present the findings to a team, including the victim of the bullying.

Research has shown that restorative justice meets the needs of victims, reduces the frequency of reoffending, and can positively impact the school's truancy and suspension rates. If your school does not have a formal restorative justice program, you can easily educate yourself and implement a modified version in your own class. I have listed some resources at the end of the book.

Even the younger students can fill out a reflection sheet with words and drawings to identify their thoughts and feelings before an incident and recognize the harmful effect the behavior had on others.

COMMUNICATION

Effective, non-reactionary communication is a crucial element of all aspects of classroom management. But here are some specifics to keep in mind.

Do not repeat yourself Make an explicit request of the behavior you want to see, remind the student of the consequences of not producing that behavior, and move on. Do not try and convince students to behave. In general, the less you say, the better.

One rule that has served me well in parenting and in teaching is to keep my requests to "under ten words and under ten seconds."

Do not engage in discussion with a student about their behavior. As I mentioned previously, participating in an argument or even a conversation with a student about their behavior is a no-win situation. It will waste class time, distract others, and this situation can needlessly escalate as the student tries to save face in front of their peers. If a student decides to argue with you, you can validate their feelings but then let them know that if they want to continue the conversation, they need to do it on their own time after class. This is not just so you hope they will have forgotten about the incident by then, but it also gives you both a chance to revisit the situation when emotions have calmed down. Validating can be as easy as saying, *"I understand. But the rule is…"*

Also, get comfortable calmly saying,

"We have finished talking about this. If you want to tell me more, please stay in at recess, and we can discuss the rule further."

Use as much non-verbal communication to manage behavior as possible such as using hand gestures, handing out tickets, standing by particular students, and quietly assigning or removing individual or table points.

One effective strategy I used when substitute teaching was to write "Recess" or similar on the board and silently walk over and just erase a letter if the class as a whole was not on task. I didn't even need to say anything, but students would notice and quickly correct their behavior most of the time. Of course, you can also use the same strategy for positive rewards. The teacher putting marbles in a jar for positive behavior is a tried and true elementary school strategy. The goal is for the class to earn an agreed-upon reward such as a pizza party or extra recess once the jar is full.

Be respectful and confident, and avoid personal comments Remember that the behavior is the problem, not the student. Stick with, "The rule is to stay in your seat while I'm talking," not "You got out of your seat".

Avoid using absolutes such as "always" or "never" No one "always" does anything. "You always disrupt the class" has a very accusatory tone to it. Students will legitimately feel that you are picking on them.

Delete sarcasm and rhetorical questions from your communication repertoire in the classroom. They are subtly damaging and unproductive.

A good rule for all relationships is to **keep the ratio of positive comments to negative ones at least five to one**. That means for every time you criticize a child's choice, you should make an effort to catch them doing something right at least five times. "I like the way you handled that!" or slipping them a ticket as you pass by and they are on task takes very little time but makes considerable deposits in their emotional bank accounts. They will feel less likely to be targeted for their negative behavior. Negative messages inspire resistance, while positive ones inspire cooperation and confidence.

Communicate to students that you have high academic expectations for all of them and that you are confident that they can achieve them. You may be aware of studies that prove a direct correlation between teacher expectations and student achievement. One study tells the tale of two teachers who accidentally received reversed class lists. One teacher was told they had very high achieving students, and told the students as much and treated them as such. In fact, they were a class of lower-achieving students, but rose to the occasion and outperformed the "real" super achievers. Those students were placed with a teacher who had been told they had the lower ability students. This presumably was before the days of summative tests and heterogeneous class grouping, but you get my point. We need to have high expectations for all of our students and communicate to them that we have confidence that they can achieve.

CHEERFULNESS

As a teacher, your energy speaks louder than your words. When we reflect on our own school experience, our favorite teachers and the classes where we learned the most were probably the ones where the teacher was passionate, engaging, and yes, cheerful.

If channeling your inner Mary Poppins isn't your thing, being quietly cheerful and positive is also okay. What does not deliver a productive educational experience is a continuously exhausted, frustrated teacher who is overwhelmed and burnt out. That's not to say we can't have a bad day, everyone has those. But if the vibe we emit is consistently that we would rather be anywhere else but in the classroom, we will have constant classroom management issues.

Students are very sensitive to energy. As mentioned earlier, they have good "fake" detectors. They can sense if we value them and their opinions and if we enjoy being around them. They know if we are truly trying to understand their issues, help them grow and learn, or if we are just demanding compliance.

Negative energy becomes a vicious circle. Poor classroom management skills lead to behavior problems, which negatively impacts the teacher and the students. The teacher becomes increasingly overwhelmed, worn out, lacking confidence in their abilities, and their classroom management suffers, which again exacerbates the problem. It can become a circle of shame and blame and misery. The opposite of the class "vibe" we all desire - collaboration, cooperation, high student engagement, and successful learning outcomes.

This entire book is aimed at reducing teacher overwhelm. While it is not always possible to change our natural disposition, the mindset habits at the beginning of this book should help us bring the best of ourselves to our students every day.

Make a conscious effort to avoid the energy vampires on campus and the group of professional complainers who congregate in various places. Take self-care seriously, and be protective of your own energy. Both you and your students deserve to have a positive experience together every day.

While I do advocate for a calm teaching style, that does not always mean the energy in your room needs to be quiet.

Whenever possible, find a way to inject some fun into your learning. If you feel like the class is dragging, get up and have a dance party! Even older students will appreciate being allowed to vote on a school appropriate song to blast in class for a few minutes to boost the mood.

Finding ways to have fun and laugh with your class is one of the most natural paths to building a class community. While it's important to set appropriate limits on being too friendly with students, it's not true that you should value being respected over being liked. You should be both. As noted here,

---

"Kids don't learn from people they don't like."

Rita Pierson TED Talk Every Kid Needs a Champion

A SIDE NOTE **on apologizing**

We are all human, and we work in a field that is often very stressful. The days are dynamic, and often, situations come up that we did not anticipate or prepare for. That's part of what makes teaching exciting, but also what makes it challenging. There will be times that we raise our voice to a class, or don't handle a situation with a student the way we would have liked. In those times, it is important to apologize.

I know educators who think that their students will lose respect for them if they apologize but, in my experience, the opposite is true. It's not like students don't notice that you have just yelled and are frustrated. When things are calm, you should model the appropriate behavior by apologizing.

There is nothing wrong with saying to a class, "I'm sorry that I raised my voice before, you know that I don't like to talk to you that way. I'm not feeling great today, and I let my frustration get the better of me. I apologize. Thanks for understanding."

Messing up once in a while is inevitable. If it becomes a pattern, we should take responsibility as professionals and ask our administrator for some extra training or coaching in specific areas we are lacking.

Now let's take those seven foundational Cs, and examine how we can set up our classroom rules and expectations at the beginning of the year, in class and online.

Standards versus Rules

Much has been written about setting up class rules. Usually, the advice is to:

- Limit them to no more than five
- Make sure they are phrased in the positive. That means that the rule dictates the behavior you want versus the one that you don't. So the rule would be, "Stay in your seat," not "Don't get out of your seat."

- Ensure they are posted where everyone can see them - possibly have students sign a poster of the rules or take home a copy for signature.
- Ensure you have a consistent escalation procedure for when the rules are broken. For example, first a verbal warning or move your clip, an in-class consequence, then a phone call home, and finally a referral to administration. Extreme behavior or aggression usually results in an immediate trip to the office.

These are all good protocols. However, for the last six years, I have worked with the idea of "Class Standards" instead of rules to build community. The conversation becomes about, "What type of learning environment do we want to be in every day?" and the standards support that.

While I am the one to determine the standards, I invite student input by asking,

"What does that look like?"

"What does that mean to you?"

so that they feel involved in the process. I also distinguish between our class procedures (how we do things) and class standards (how we conduct ourselves).

I give the students plenty of time to provide input on our procedures. This gives them a voice, even if they don't get a choice in the standards.

The standards I use are modified from a Project GLAD (Guided Language Acquisition Instruction) training our school participated in. I only have four.

1. Show respect
2. Make good decisions
3. Solve the problem
4. Take responsibility for your own learning

These four standards are general enough to be all-encompassing and to encapsulate all the positive behaviors I want to see. Even though the students don't play an active role in deciding the standards, I secure their "buy-in" and allow them to use their voice by having discussions such as,

"What kind of learning environment do you want to be in?"

"What behaviors make you feel safe in learning?"

"Do you enjoy being in a class where everyone is cooperating, and you get to work together and help each other grow?"

"Would you rather be learning, or listening to the teacher nagging and having to talk to students about their behavior?"

I make sure that students are clear on the "why" of the standards. The standards are for their benefit. They ensure that the classroom is an orderly, friendly, safe place for them to learn. I assure students that I will consistently and fairly enforce the standards so that minimal time is wasted with distractions and there is more time for learning and fun. First comes the work, then comes the fun. If time is lost because I am managing behavior, the whole class loses, and that's not fair.

I positively set the tone for high achievement in learning and also for behavior. I let students know that I believe they are all capable of achieving at high academic levels and controlling themselves so that they can all be cooperative, productive members of our class community.

A quick note on looking at students' previous track records

Unless a student has a specialized learning plan or accommodations that I need to be aware of, I make a conscious effort not to look at students' cumulative files or comments that previous teachers make about their behavior. I like to give every student a "clean slate".

Just because a student has behaved a certain way for a previous teacher, it does not mean that they will necessarily behave that way for me. Maybe the student has matured. Perhaps I have a different style than the previous teacher, which inspires better choices from the child. Perhaps that student really just needed a fresh start.

I can't think of anything more demoralizing for a student to show up in a new grade with a new teacher and already find themselves sitting in isolation because of the teacher's preconceived idea of how they will behave in their class. I have seen this many times, and I find it very sad. Please do not set up a student to fail that way. It sends the opposite message of what we should be communicating which is:

"I believe in you and your ability to bring the best of yourself to this class."

Hand Signals

At the beginning of the year, the students and I practice repeating the standards with our voices and our fingers. Here's what I mean by that. We put our right arm out front, and when repeating "show respect", we touch the index finger to the thumb. When we say, "make good decisions", we touch the middle finger to the thumb. When we say, "solve the problem", we touch the ring finger to the thumb. And when we say "take responsibility for your own learning", we touch the little finger to the thumb. We practice the standards touching our fingers repeatedly until it is automatic. Why do we do this?

The reason for touching the fingers in a specific way is two-fold. First, using TPR (total physical response) engages both hemispheres of the brain and facilitates memorization. Second, it allows me to manage behavior without talking and interrupting the flow of my teaching.

For example, if a student is whispering to a friend while I am giving instruction, once I make eye contact with them, I need only touch my index finger to my thumb without saying anything, and the student knows I am redirecting them by reminding them to "show respect". If I am working with a small group and a student comes up to me to ask a procedural question or for something readily available somewhere else in the room, I need only touch my ring finger to my thumb without saying anything. The student knows I'm telling them they have the ability to solve their own problem.

As much as possible, I like to use hand signals to redirect student behavior without talking. Doing so is less likely to take me out of my flow and distract other students. It also sends a clear message that I will not be stopping my teaching to engage with them.

It is also helpful to teach students hand signals. It is very irritating to ask a question of your class and pick on a student with a raised arm only to hear not the answer to that question, but a request such as "May I go to the bathroom?" or a comment.

We practice hand signals at the beginning of the year, and I have small posters on the wall to remind them of the common ones. We have hand signals for:

- Needing to go to the bathroom
- Needing to have a drink of water
- Needing a pencil
- Needing a tissue

Having hand signals for these everyday requests means that I can simply nod at a student and let them know they may get what they need, or I can raise my index finger to indicate, "Hang on a minute until it's a better time."

My favorite hand signals to teach are the ones that are in response to a question I've posed.

If a student has an **answer to a question**, they raise their thumb.

If a student has **a comment**, they make their hand into a "C" shape.

If a student **has a question**, they raise their little finger.

In this way, I can better control the flow of discussions. No more calling on a student with a raid hand to answer a question and hearing, "*Is it lunchtime yet?*"

We make a game of practicing and have fun with it. Pretty soon into the year, if a student just puts their hand in the air I tell them, "I don't know a hand in the air means."

These are all standard hand signals. I believe the first time I saw them was at a classroom management seminar by Rick Morris. Posters for these hand signals are easily found on the Internet. Many teachers use them. I am always so pleased when students come into my classroom already knowing how to use them from previous grades.

This Signals/Checking For Understanding

I also use hand signals for checking for understanding. Thumbs up means the student understands, a sideways thumb means they almost have it, and a thumbs down means the student needs more explanation. When checking for understanding, I make students use their thumb signals up against their chest so as not to be visible to the whole class. Students also wait to show me until they are prompted so that everybody does it at the same time. My prompt is, *"Ready, set, show me!"*

These two procedures ensure authentic responses and that students don't feel self-conscious if they need more help because it is not a public broadcast.

I use a prompt for all checking for understanding, even whiteboards. I use combination clipboard/whiteboards in class. The reverse side is gray, so my prompt is "Gray when ready." That prompts students to hold up the side that doesn't have the answer when they are ready. Once I see most students are ready, I go ahead with "Ready, set, show me!" This discourages students from simply copying the answers of other students they know are likely to have the correct answer.

The essential idea for the first weeks of school is to practice, practice, practice! Practice all of the rules or standards, procedures, and routines. Have fun with it! Role-play. Students love it when I designate a teacher and I play the role of a student with goofy or outrageous behavior.

Self-Managing Routines

One of the most effective ways of reducing teacher overwhelm is to establish self-managing routines in the classroom. It is worth investing time in this at the beginning of the year as, again, it will save you time and frustration in the long run.

Students should know how to transition between tasks, what to do when they are done with their work, and what to do if they need help. This is especially important if you work in small groups or have any types of rotations in class. But any repeated activity such as lining up, walking in an orderly line, taking out and returning devices, and cleaning up the room for the end of the day should all have a clear, well-rehearsed routine.

The more you can train students to be responsible for taking out, distributing, organizing, and returning materials, the more smoothly the day will go. Students love to help! Even students who are too old for a cutesy "Jobs Chart" on the wall can be assigned roles on a rotating basis.

It is worth taking time to evaluate all the things that you do as a teacher during the day and determining if any of them can reasonably be outsourced to students. Even if I have to accept that not everything will be done as well as you would have done it, I will take an "outsourced" job over a perfect one any day. If it takes me five minutes to make that collected and sorted pile of perfect papers versus 15 minutes it would have taken me to do the whole task myself, I still saved myself 10 minutes. 10 minutes five days a week is almost an entire hour you have to spend on tasks that more directly impact student learning.

As the saying goes, *"Don't let perfect be the enemy of good."*

Distance Learning Classroom Management

Luckily, many of the same strategies apply to manage behavior in the distance learning environment.

If we are working with a hybrid model or started in the classroom and then had to pivot to online, learning the standards and hand gestures would be part of the students' natural routines. However, clear guidelines for online behavior expectations would need to be explicitly taught and practiced as if it were the beginning of the year.

Live video-conferencing has its own set of classroom management challenges. Although teachers joke how great it is to be able to "mute" students, it's very hard to enforce overall engagement and compliance. If a student chooses to turn off their camera and not participate, there is little recourse we have at that moment.

Developing a list of agreed-upon guidelines for participation shouldn't be a chore. Just as if you were in the classroom, have fun and role play. Practice! Assign a "teacher" and take on the role of a student and model appropriate and inappropriate behavior. Remind students of the "why". We all want to be in an environment where we can learn.

I tell students wasting precious time when we are all together in a live environment is the same as "stealing learning" from our friends. That probably isn't appropriate for older students, but it makes a powerful impression on younger students. I also incentivize them to stay on task. If I schedule an hour for our call and get through the work in 50 minutes, they have 10 minutes to "hang out and chat" with their friends. I stay on the call to monitor appropriateness, but I put myself on mute and off camera and just continue with my work on another browser.

Naturally, this is less of an incentive for older students who can chat with each other on social media, but for younger students who like to see their friends, it can help.

If you are only providing distance learning, then you will need to invest time upfront in establishing the class standards and the reason behind them. I also recommend that you teach the hand gestures for checking for understanding, as well as the gestures for, "I have an answer," "I have a comment", and "I have a question."

In participating in live video conferencing with multiple students, one of the class rules will probably be to have your microphone on "mute" unless you are called on. Having students use hand gestures is very useful. Knowing if the student has an answer, a comment, or a question is a lot more meaningful to a teacher than merely saying seeing the raised hand icon or a student's actual raised hand on the screen.

Hand gestures are also an easy way to check for understanding. Remember to use the prompt "Ready, set, show me!" before students show their thumbs. Although in video conferencing, obviously, all the students will be able to see how their peers answered.

Just as in the classroom, one of the best ways to minimize behavior problems is to provide engaging content and activities and ensure that the "vibe" is positive and upbeat. If we have done an adequate job of creating a real class community as outlined in the previous chapter, students will be more inclined to participate and self regulate. If we can give those students who crave attention lots of positive reinforcement outside of the live video conferences, this will also help reduce time wasted on redirecting behavior.

I adopt the mindset that if a student truly does not want to participate or learn, I don't stress if they don't show up to a Zoom call. If I am recording the live video meeting, they can watch it later at their own convenience. It's better that the student does not show than show up and distract others. It helps to remember the mindset of focus on what we can control. Don't let the one student who is "missing in action" detract from you being present with the other twenty students who did show up. You will have time after the call to reach out to the student.

So far, in these two sections, we have looked at the mindsets and practical strategies for setting ourselves up for success. Managing all of the moving components in any school year is challenging. When we are dealing with juggling online and classroom learning, even more so.

In the last section, I will give suggestions and best practices for managing all of the moving parts without getting burnt out. I will also explain the single most useful piece of advice I have ever received. It has helped manage my stress, transform my relationships with students, and keep true to my teaching North Star. I'm so excited to share it with you!

Part III

OVERCOMING TEACHER OVERWHELM

5

Surviving Teacher Overwhelm

NEXT TIME you are having trouble falling asleep, instead of counting sheep, try making a mental list of all the things teachers are expected to do on a day to day basis. You will probably drift off before you get to the bottom of the list.

Below is a highlight of what most teachers cram into a regular day. I'm sure there is more that is missing, but this is a start.

- Design and present academically rigorous instruction that supports student learning
- Select, administer, grade and interpret summative and formative assessments
- Analyze the data and differentiate instruction based on the results of the assessments
- Grade work and provide relevant, individualized feedback
- Track, record and communicate grades
- Provide, collect (chase down), and grade homework. Track more grades
- Effectively manage classroom behavior
- Resolve student conflicts
- Attend to students' social and emotional needs and

development, including crisis response and fulfilling the duties of being a mandated reporter

- Provide troubleshooting for technical issues with student devices (assuming they all brought them and they are charged)
- Communicate with parents (parent conferences, phone calls, emails, and tech support)
- Plan and communicate with colleagues
- Cover yard, lunch, and end of day dismissal duty
- Participate in meetings - staff meetings, grade span meetings, committee meetings, parent/teacher meeting, student study team meetings, and IEP (special education) meetings (so many meetings!)
- Report on data (so much data!)
- Organize educational field trips, and, in most cases, fundraise to pay for them

This list doesn't even include adjunct duties or volunteer after school assignments such as theater, art, band, athletics, science fairs, school newspaper, yearbook and even more meetings for committees we are pressured to volunteer for (there's a verb for that, it's "voluntold").

Much like Marzano's research that calculated it would take 22 years of instructional minutes to cover the required content standards, it would probably take even the most efficient of professional educators a minimum of twelve hours a day, every day, to complete all of these responsibilities effectively. Just the first two items of the list are more than enough for an entire job description. Add to this the time we spend commuting to work, and tending to our children, families, and home responsibilities. It's no wonder that even the most dedicated and passionate teachers spend so much time in a state of overwhelm, exhaustion, frustration and insecurity that they are simply not giving any area of their life enough attention.

It often feels that in struggling to do everything, we don't do anything as well as we should. No matter how hard we work, some area of our life feels that it's getting neglected. Especially recently, it feels that more is added to the list, not less. It's no wonder that many teachers are burnt out and leaving the profession in droves. It's both a complicated issue and a simple math equation- there just aren't enough hours in the day to do it all well.

Although this paints a bleak picture, the fact remains that as professionals, we need to take responsibility and manage our own schedules and priorities. Nobody is going to give us permission to do less. And while there are times that a large amount of "extra hours" are required, an extreme example being during Shelter in Place, consistently working extra long hours is not sustainable. We need to find a way to proactively manage our time and responsibilities so that when we interact with students, they get the best of us.

I have seen numerous versions of this meme:

"On a day to day basis, teachers make as many decisions as surgeons."

While that statement is anecdotal, no teacher would deny the truth of it. Managing the dynamics and moving components in a classroom requires constant decision making. After years of classroom experience, I can make many of these decisions instinctively, but it is still mentally taxing. If we are exhausted and overwhelmed, it is hard to make quick and effective judgment calls. In worst case scenarios, when a student is in crisis, or unpredictable outside factors are in play, poor decisions will affect student safety. In non-critical situations, ineffective decisions can still result in more problems, increased stress, and more overwhelm, which becomes one big vicious cycle.

Although it is a term initially coined by Richard Boyatzis and Annie McKee in the context of leaders in the business world, "Sacrifice Syndrome", where professionals live in constant crisis mode without taking time for self-renewal, is highly prevalent in the teacher world. Students need capable and caring adults to tend to their social and emotional needs now more than ever. It's hard for us to bring the best of ourselves to our students if we're depleted and running on empty. It is also incumbent on us to model healthy habits.

Learning to tackle that overwhelm, even if it means ultimately doing less, is not selfish; it's absolutely necessary.

Paradoxically, when we are strategic about our activities and setting boundaries around our time, we will ultimately be more effective and more productive. Schools are full of busy people. Our goal is not to be busy, but to be effective and focus on the things that truly matter in terms of student outcomes and our own happiness.

Here are some practical mindsets and strategies to help accomplish this.

Give Yourself Permission to Do Less

I talked about this earlier in the mindset section, but it's important enough to repeat. When situations are uncertain and plans are frequently changing, it's helpful to assume the best intentions of others or allow them grace. Often, the expectations for teachers are simply unrealistic. Think of teachers who were tasked with providing remote teaching from their homes. Many had no training and only one day to prep. Many also had young children of their own running around who needed parental supervision and assistance with their learning. It was an impossible task.

We extend grace to others, and we need to also extend it to ourselves. Not every lesson is going to be Pinterest perfect. Not every email is going to get an immediate response (nor should it). Sometimes it's best to accept that we are doing the best we can in the situation we find ourselves in and not beat ourselves up if every lesson doesn't hit the eight critical elements of lesson design. Some days merely doing our best is going to have to be good enough.

So that's the first mindset: let yourself off the hook. I'm guessing that most teachers on their worst days still get more done than most people practicing other professions.

Work Smarter, Not Harder

In The First Days of School, Harry Wong recommended that teachers become adept at "Beg, borrow, and steal." What he meant by that is that even though instructional practices change, there are still some fundamentals such as reading, writing, and arithmetic that have not changed.

It's unlikely that what you are actually trying to teach has never been taught before, even if we may be using different technology or instructional practices to explain it. Somebody out there in the teaching universe has already prepared a lesson. Ideally, that person will be on your campus. If not, I'm sure the magic of Google can find it for you somewhere.

I'm not suggesting you steal other people's work or ideas- give credit where credit is due. But don't reinvent the wheel just for the sake of it.

Hopefully, you are part of a grade level team that collaborates well, even if it has to be virtually. While my own team is fantastic about sharing resources and supporting each other during shelter in place distance learning, if we needed to provide distance or blended learning for a more extended period of time, we would all benefit from being more strategic in our planning. As there are four of us and four major content areas, it would make sense for each of us to plan for one content area and share resources. We could rotate content areas weekly or bi-weekly to ensure no one gets "stuck" with their least favorite content area.

CURRENTLY, I work with talented and dedicated professionals and, although we have different teaching styles, we are all focused on student results. We work well together and leverage each other's strengths and take into account everybody's different levels of home responsibilities when delegating responsibilities. I admit this is a dream scenario that is not a reality for all teachers. There was a ten year period in my teaching career when I was a "lone warrior", and I had to find my teaching friends outside of my school campus.

It is hard to teach in isolation. Make it a priority to seek out online communities of teachers who teach similar grade levels or content if you aren't part of a dream team. When I go to conferences or professional development classes, I always make connections with seemingly like-minded educators. It can be beneficial to maintain relationships with mentors and teaching friends outside of your immediate circle of colleagues. They can provide perspective, support, and impartial advice, especially when dealing with campus politics and drama.

Sometimes when we are overwhelmed and short on time, the path of least resistance is simply to purchase pre-made resources or digital units that you can modify to your immediate needs without too much effort. There's no shame in heading over to TeachersPayTeachers.com to either browse for ideas or purchase inexpensive resources.

Recognize Who Your True Competition Is

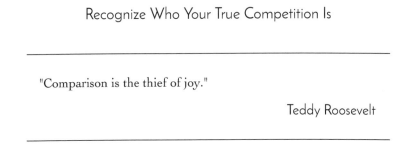

"Comparison is the thief of joy."

Teddy Roosevelt

EVERYBODY'S SITUATION IS UNIQUE. Some of us are new to teaching while others are veterans. Some teachers have been successfully implementing blended learning for years. Others are struggling to remember our Google Classroom password and freeze in front of the YouTube Live camera. Some of us have young children at home that demand much of our time and attention. Others don't. It's best not to compare what you're doing with what you see on the internet or being bragged about at staff meetings.

Again, we can learn and borrow from others, but that's different from the insecurity that comes from comparing what we're doing to others who seem to be doing it all effortlessly. Remember that people usually post their successes on social media, not things that didn't go well or were simply okay. It's an idealized version of what they are doing, not necessarily a reflection of the truth.

A teacher's goal is not to accumulate "likes" or accolades, but to provide connection and instruction that positively affects student outcomes. New educational software and learning tools can seem very exciting, but we don't need to chase every new shiny looking toy.

This is what helps.

When evaluating your efforts, stick with the fundamental questions:

- Are students engaged?
- Are they persevering and problem-solving?
- Are they able to demonstrate mastery of the skill?
- Are they collaborating and having fun?

These are the criteria you should use to measure your efforts and results, not how Pinterest, Facebook, or Instagram worthy they are or whether or not they will impress your colleagues.

Our "why" of teaching isn't to impress other adults. It's to positively impact children. It helps to adopt the mindset that our competition isn't other people, but that our competition is ourselves. Our goal should be to be the best version of ourselves - better teachers, friends, parents, and members of society compared to the person we were yesterday, not in comparison to other people or other teachers. Everyone's journey is different.

Set Boundaries on Your Space

One challenge created by advancements in technology is that the boundaries between "work space" and "home space" have become blurred. Even though teachers have always brought assignments and assessments home to grade, our communication with others about school matters mostly happened at work. It used to be if parents, students, administrators, and co-workers wanted to talk to us or demand something of us they needed to do so at school, during school hours. Now we have the persistent pinging of email notifications and texts until the moment we go to bed.

On campus, most of our day is spent with classroom instruction, working with students in groups, or one on one intervention. Because we use our time on campus to work directly with students, other responsibilities such as lesson planning, electronic communication and paperwork/reports need to happen outside of school hours.

The good news is that with everything being available on our laptops, we no longer need to stay at school until ridiculously late. We can easily bring it home with us. The bad news is that when we bring it all home, it's hard for us to fully step away from it and refresh and recharge.

Here are some strategies to help you set up physical and mental boundaries so that your home can be a place of relaxation, comfort, and enjoying quality time with our family can be a priority.

First, if possible, designate just one area of your home for the purpose of working. This is especially important if we are engaged in providing distance learning from home. If our laptop and curriculum are spread all over the kitchen table, it's especially hard to separate work from home. Few of us have designated home offices. It's important to find one small space that you can dedicate to working.

When I was providing distance learning from home, I set up a table in the hallway with a large folding partition separating my area from my son's bedroom behind it. My son knew if the partition was up, I was working and not to disturb me. Of course, my son is not a toddler or a young child demanding constant attention. I understand that not all of us have the luxury of putting up a "do not disturb" sign. But whenever possible, set up at least one small area designated to work. It's hard to truly relax in your kitchen or on your sofa if your laptop is sitting right there.

Next, if you are teaching from campus, try to complete as much work there as possible, even if it means staying a little later. As I do not have young children I need to attend to, I have a lot of flexibility in how much time I spend on campus. I prefer to leave work at work. I set up a schedule where two days a week, I go in early, and one night a week, I stay extra late to complete lesson planning, grading, and reports. If I have nothing mission-critical to achieve at night, I leave my work tote in the garage. I don't even bring it into the house.

To complete all of my work at work, I often have to forgo things like spending my lunchtime in the staff room or chatting with colleagues after work. To me, it's worth it to feel I have more balance in my life. I prefer to stay late one night a week and feel that I have three or four evenings left a week to pursue things that interest me that are not related to school.

Have a "Closing Ritual"

Whether at work or home, develop a closing ritual. Power down your computer or laptop and clear up your desk. I like to leave a bright sticky note with the top priorities for the next day written on my desk. It sends a message to my brain that everything is in good order, and I can pick it up again tomorrow. There is no need to worry about things I need to do tomorrow when I'm at home and can do nothing about them.

My favorite closing ritual is to write in my Positive Mindset Journal For Teachers before I go home. I jot down my favorite three things of the day and think of someone I can thank or champion in the morning. Intentionally tuning our mental radar to the positive is so important.

A free PDF copy of the journal that you can print out and write in is available at the link I provided at the beginning of the book. I especially like writing down my "three best things" right before I go home so that the first person who asks me how my day was gets to hear the good stuff, not the drama and frustrations.

Set Boundaries on Your Time (and Stick to Them)

Like many people, I have a love/hate relationship with technology. I love that I can virtually visit with my 84-year-old mother who lives alone on the other side of the world every day. It seems a miracle that I can hang out with her in her kitchen despite a 5,000 mile and 8 hour time difference.

I can't imagine how difficult it is for teachers to provide distance teaching without technology. While video conferencing and sharing assignments and feedback digitally aren't ideal, they still provide an opportunity for connection and direct help, unlike a packet of papers sent home. Instead of throwing my back out, dragging home massive teacher editions, books, and papers, technology allows me to access it on one small device. For those who grew up having to go to the library and dig through encyclopedias for information as a child, having the entire content of human knowledge available to us on a phone in our pocket seems almost unbelievable. I have degrees in two foreign languages. Do you have any idea how heavy and expensive foreign language dictionaries used to be? Technology rocks!

That's the love part.

The hate part? We are never really "off" from work. People can contact us via text message, phone call, or email 24 hours a day.

Here are some strategies to help set boundaries around our time that can help.

First, manage expectations. Whether Back To School Night is in the classroom or virtually, present a clear plan of how parents should contact you. Explain that your duties do not end with the dismissal bell and that if parents want to meet with you in person, it will be hard to give them the time and attention they need without an appointment. Nobody likes to be hijacked at their door right before school or at the end of the day. When providing distance learning, publish your "office hours" when you will be readily available. Then manage the expectation as to when parents can expect a reply to questions. I always say I'll reply within one school day, although most times I get back to people by the end of the day, even if it's just to let them know I have received their correspondence and am working on a solution.

Next, recognize that just because someone contacts you outside of the school day, they don't necessarily expect an immediate response. Many people email you when they finally get done with their other responsibilities and want to send the message before they forget. They are not necessarily expecting an immediate reply. I have been guilty of this. I remember one Sunday evening when I was finishing up lesson planning, I had a question for our curriculum team, and I emailed it. I was mortified when 8 o'clock on a Sunday night, the curriculum coordinator, who I know has two small children at home, responded to my email. I hadn't been expecting a reply, I just wanted to send the email while it was on my mind because I know Monday mornings are always a rush before school.

So remember that people often send emails when it's convenient for them without any "sub text" that they expect you to be always available.

Leveraging technology can also work to your advantage. I mentioned before that I use a parent communication app called Class Dojo. I like it because it's on my phone and I can send messages, post class information and receive texts without giving out my personal phone number. Most apps of this nature allow you to set "do not disturb" hours. This means then that even though a parent can message you at any time, you will only receive a notification if the communication occurred within your specified available hours. Of course, if you want to proactively check the messages, you can at any time, but there is no risk of being disturbed on your downtime unless you choose to be.

When I was providing distance teaching from home, there were many times that I wanted to communicate with the parents by phone. If you have a Gmail account, you can get a free Google voice number. This is a local phone number that will allow you to make phone calls from an app on your phone. This way you have the convenience of talking to parents without revealing your personal phone number. The fact that it is based on an app means you can choose to look at it when it is convenient for you without getting automatic notifications. It is a free service, and there are many other apps that you can also use the same way.

Get Comfortable Declining Requests

"Working hard on something you don't want to do is called stress. Working hard on something you do want to do is called passion."

Simon Sinek

Besides our multitude of regular responsibilities, most educators have adjunct duties and are also involved with after school enrichment activities for students. When volunteering for such duties, it makes sense to focus on things that we enjoy. For me, that's always going to involve activities where I work directly with students.

Here's an example. For 15 years, I was the coordinator for an interactive planetarium at our school. I needed to drive 50 miles to pick up the equipment after school on a Friday night, come in early on a Monday to set it all up, provide lesson plans for a substitute to teach my own class for a week, and put on a family astronomy night until nine o'clock in the evening during the week. After our weekly staff meeting on Friday afternoon, I would pack up the equipment and drive 50 miles to return it.

Needless to say, it was a lot of extra work for me. Did I mention the dome weighed about 80 lbs and the computer to run the planetarium about the same? I did this on a purely voluntary zero stipend basis.

However, it was by far one of the most favorite parts of my year.

I worked at a small school, and during Astronomy Week I interacted with almost every student. Students were excited to crawl into a huge dome, see the night sky, and learn about constellations, planets, and phases of the moon. They would often grab me as I walked across the playground and ask, "Mrs. S, when is it time for StarLab?"

Watching the excitement on their faces and hearing all the "oohs" and "ahhs" in the dark was a thoroughly rewarding experience. Being part of a committee that "unpacked" the new science content framework (a document the size of a phone book) ad nauseam at monthly meetings after school was much less rewarding. In fact, I'd go so far as to say they were what I call "ice pick" meetings. There were times I felt I would rather poke myself in the eye with an ice pack than sit through one of those meetings for five more minutes.

You get my point. If we love a sport or theater, spending hours coaching or putting on a play will fill us up, not deplete us.

What happens if we are directly asked to volunteer for something that doesn't interest us, or something that just comes at a bad time when we have too many other commitments on our plate? We need to get comfortable with graciously declining.

Saying "no" does not come naturally for many educators. Unfortunately, many of us have bought into a narrative that says teachers who are constantly seen on campus or volunteering for all activities work harder, care more about students, and are better teachers. We care about how we are perceived by parents and administrators and often feel pressured to do things we don't really want to do outside of scheduled hours. The result is often additional stress and resentment, which definitely does NOT make us better teachers or any more pleasant to live with.

If we find ourselves continually saying yes to things that we do not really want to do, we may work at a school that fosters a culture of measuring teacher value not by student engagement and outcomes, but by hours spent on campus. If this is your situation, I encourage you to be strategic about the activities you agree to take. Focus on positions with the shortest time commitment while making you visible to key stakeholders such as parents and administrators. This also falls under the heading of working smarter, not harder.

It can be especially hard to decline requests if we are caught off guard or asked by someone we report to. The best strategy for this is to buy ourselves some time. We need to get comfortable with saying,

"Thanks for thinking of me. Let me check my schedule and get back to you,"

or,

"Let me give the matter some thought and get back to you."

I always recommend responding via email or text. This can eliminate the awkwardness of having to decline in person. Additionally, we will have documentation that we declined in the event we ever need it.

Of course, we should decline graciously. If a colleague or parent is inviting us to participate in something, it is perfectly acceptable to say that we have a previous conflicting engagement. We do not need to feel obligated to disclose what it is. And we certainly don't need to apologize or say, "I'm sorry."

"Unfortunately, I'm unable to help you with that. But thanks for thinking of me and good luck with the project!"

is a perfectly acceptable answer.

This is important! If an administrator or superior asks you, be sure to give a reason that is *student focused*. For example,

"I really have my plate full with the new curriculum/grade level/whatever else you can think of this year, and I'm reluctant to take on any additional duties that take me away from my students,"

or,

"I have a lot of students who need extra help this year, and I need to devote whatever extra time I have to helping them be successful."

Set Up a Routine

Another powerful productivity strategy is to set up a schedule to work on routine tasks that are similar. For example, I usually stay late on a Wednesday and do the lesson planning for the following week. During the week, I put aside any ideas or lessons I've found and wait until Wednesday to evaluate them and see how/if they fit in.

I give weekly quizzes that need to be graded on Friday mornings, right before our weekly PE lesson. I take a chair out to the playground and score the quizzes right during PE, knowing that if I stay in my room, I will lose that potential 40-minute block to checking emails, tidying up, and surfing the internet and will be irritated that I have to grade them on the weekend. Immediately grading the quizzes means I can set up my small group instruction and reteaching groups for the following week during Friday lunchtime, and make all of the copies I need Friday right after school.

My class also has a music class once a week on Mondays. I go with them to the music room with my laptop and spend the 40 minutes entering grades. Again, if I stayed in my room, I would be open to unscheduled interruptions and distractions.

Having a schedule and routine helps with "single-tasking" (more on that next) and also relieves stress. Instead of having lesson planning, correcting, and entering grades constantly hanging over my head, I remind myself, "I will do that on Monday" or whatever the designated day is.

Having a schedule also helps to keep less preferred tasks from piling up. You may be aware of the saying, "It's easier to keep up than catch up!" This is especially true for tasks such as correcting papers and entering grades.

When You're Working - Really Work

Being busy is not the same as being productive. We often put in really long days at school, only to drag work home with us feeling that we are getting increasingly behind. Making progress on our to-do list can seem frustratingly difficult.

I have often transported the same set of papers to grade back and forth so many places with me that I felt they should have their own passports. All schools are mandated to provide break times and a planning or prep period. Why does it often feel like no "work" such as planning and grading can happen at work?

One reason is that we are not proactive enough about protecting our planning time. Some responsibilities unexpectedly crop up over which we have little control- meetings with parents or administrators and discipline issues that need to be addressed outside classroom time are just a few examples. But many times, our planning period gets hijacked by a colleague who steps into the classroom to ask a question or borrow something and ends up chatting or complaining for the entire time. We're lucky if the only thing we accomplished during our precious prep is a quick trip to the bathroom.

It can be the same with our lunch period. We have things we need or want to accomplish but pop into the staff room to make a copy or heat up our lunch, then end up chatting until the bell goes and we have to literally run back to our classrooms.

If your classroom is in a busy location, you might have to consider doing your prep work elsewhere. I once had a classroom that was on the traffic path to the copy machine. People were constantly walking through my room. Even if they just stopped to have a quick chat, the constant interruptions made it hard for me to get anything achieved during my prep period.

I found it was easier for me to schedule two mornings a week to come in early and one evening a week to stay late when I had the whole school wing to myself. I could focus and be very productive with no interruptions and no waiting for the copy machine or other shared equipment.

The key idea here is to be proactive in minimizing disruptions and intentional in planning a reasonable amount of time you dedicate in the week to accomplishing all your tasks.

Time Boxing and Other Productivity Hacks

So what is single-tasking? Simply put, it is the opposite of multi-tasking.

Several years ago, I wrote a book about productivity, procrastination, and research around achieving peak performance at work. Psychologists studying "dual-task interference" concluded that there are very few circumstances in which we can effectively multi-task.

We can complete repetitive tasks such as sewing, knitting, or digging while holding a conversation with no difficulties. We can sing while we cook, drive familiar routes, or shower as these are actions we can do pretty automatically. But for any task that demands focus, attention, or concentration, whether it be analytical or creative, we are being counterproductive if we multi-task. It will take us longer to accomplish anything, and our output will suffer.

So if we are checking email while on a conference call or texting and checking social media apps when lesson planning or writing a report, we don't "save" time.

Research shows that creativity and problem solving work goes through a "work cycle", much like a "sleep cycle". You may be aware that sleep happens in 90-minute cycles. To have a complete sleep cycle, our body needs to go through specific stages, from light sleep to deep sleep to REM (Rapid Eye Movement). If we are awoken at any point in the cycle, we need to go back to the beginning. Many people whose sleep is interrupted continuously by pain or breathing issues experience exhaustion because they rarely finish a complete sleep cycle.

Scientists discovered that to get to "deep work", where we are most productive, our body needs to get into a flow state. This takes time, and multi-tasking and other distractions interrupt the process. Once interrupted, we need to return to the beginning of the cycle. If we are constantly interrupted, we never get into a flow state and do our best work.

The magic number for peak productivity is 20-25 minutes of uninterrupted time. This is where the idea of time boxing comes in. It's a process to help you strategically schedule your work into 25-minute boxes.

Here are the steps:

Prioritize what you need to get done. Remember the 80/20 rule? Focus first on the 20% of activities that will produce the most significant gain.

1. Decide how much time you reasonably need to complete the task. Remember that we tend to underestimate how much time things will take, even if we eliminate distractions. So leave yourself some "wiggle room".
2. Assign the appropriate number of time boxes you will need for each task.
3. Grab a tomato! No, that's not a typo. A technique I have used for years to time box effectively and power charge my productivity is the Pomodoro technique. It was developed by an Italian economist Francesco Cirillo who used a tomato shaped kitchen timer to regulate his work into 25-minute cycles. "Pomodoro" is the Italian word for tomato.
4. After 25 minutes of distraction free work, take an intentional 5-minute break.
5. Each half-hour unit counts as one work cycle.
6. After four work cycles (two hours), take an extended break.

I use this technique all of the time. I have an app on my phone that sets the cycles and alerts me when it's time for my five-minute break. I am sure to get up, walk, stretch, and drink water in the breaks. I might plan two work cycles before school twice a week, and four work cycles for a Wednesday evening. That's eight highly focused work sessions a week, outside of my regular prep time. For most "regular" school weeks (if there is such a thing), this is enough to accomplish what I need to do.

Many free apps can do this for you. I use "Focus Keeper". I like that it has a variety of ambient sounds that I now quickly associate with highly focused work. But any timer will do. If you cannot turn off notifications on your phone, a real timer might be better so that you can remove the temptation of touching your phone altogether by removing it from your work space. Unless it's a real emergency, most messages can likely wait 25 minutes.

A great way to spend your more extended break at the end of four time boxes, or even after two, is to take a **quick brain break**.

Complete a few yoga or tai chi exercises that synchronize breath with movement. One of my favorites is "Seven Minutes of Magic" by Lee Holden. You can do it in a small space, standing, without changing your clothes. So basically, no excuses. I would love to ride my bike or go for a long walk every day, but when school is going full throttle, it can seem impossible to make the time. But seven minutes? That's very doable. Even seven minutes, if practiced consistently, can significantly reduce your stress level.

Put Your Phone in Jail

Here's something I have learned through experience. Don't use your five-minute break to "check" notifications on your phone.

Never in history have we had so many options available to us for distraction and instant gratification. Checking or sending texts and emails. Scrolling through social media accounts. A quick game of Candy Crush or Angry Birds to relax "for a minute". We can shop online, watch videos, play games, and catch up with a friend or the news cycle with a finger's flick.

The fact that we sometimes struggle to stay focused is not just because we are undisciplined and have bad habits; we are fighting against our biology. Our brains are hardwired to seek novelty. Our scrolling habit is actually addictive. Just Google "dopamine seeking reward loop" and see how many examples there are about smartphones.

We have all had the experience of "just checking social media for a minute" turn into two hours of our life that we can never get back. It's so easy to fall into a rabbit hole of distraction courtesy of Buzzfeed clickbait or YouTube's feature that automatically starts the next video.

Be disciplined about staying away from your phone if you are working. You can make "messing with phone" its own time box if you need to. Place it at the end of your deep focused work and put a strict 25-minute limit on it. Also, take advantage of such apps as the Stay Focused Chrome extension that can block social media sites when you are working.

Clean Up Your Desktop and Digital Clutter

Many of us are overwhelmed with physical and digital clutter. A time management hack I employ is something I call The Practice of Twos. Here are some of the "twos".

I set two time boxes a day for checking email—one at the beginning of the day and one at the end. If the email can be dealt with in less than two minutes, I take care of whatever I need to do, then either delete it or file it.

If you have not set up folders in your email account, please make this a top priority. Head to YouTube for directions on how to do this with whatever email service you are using. It is fairly straightforward. Never be afraid of filing your emails! Even if you forget which folder you put them in, there is an easy search feature at the top of your email to help if you need to find them later.

Anything that needs a more extended period to take care of needs to find its way into another time box, prioritized by its level of urgency. Keeping your inbox organized should keep it from feeling overwhelming and taking up more than one page on your screen. You'll be confident that the only emails in your inbox are new items or items that you need to work on. Nothing is more frustrating or a bigger waste of time than having to dig through pages of emails to find the information you need.

Invest one time box in clearing up the desktop on your computer. You will feel so much better and more productive if you put things in files and get organized. It seems like a low priority task, but a messy desk or desktop just reinforces the idea that we are overwhelmed and can't keep up every time we look at it. It's a subtle but damaging message to our subconscious mind.

I apply the same practice of twos when it comes to paper shuffling. When picking up papers from my mailbox in the staff room, I stand by the recycling bin. Anything that can be recycled doesn't even make it anywhere near my desk. Then, if the piece of paper can be dealt with in less than two minutes, I take care of it and either throw away the piece of paper or file it immediately.

I do not keep a pile of documents to be filed. The goal is to touch each piece of paper less than two times. If the piece of paper created a new project or something that cannot be dealt with in two minutes, it gets its own time box based on my schedule.

Don't Let Perfect Be the Enemy of Good

Take to heart the advice I gave in previous chapters about letting go of needing every lesson, every activity, and every handout to be perfect. 80% of the way there is often good enough. If your lesson is a great success, go back and make it perfect and add it to your library of "digital assets".

Don't be afraid of delegating just because students or a parent helper or an aide won't complete something as perfectly as you would do it.

Whenever possible, develop routines and procedures that students can run without your involvement. Capitalize on how much students enjoy helping. I have a regular crew of students who show up at my door ten minutes before school and happily organize papers and put Chromebooks and morning work on the desks. That's two fewer things that I have to do. It also gives me a few minutes of extra connection time with them as we all buzz around the room being productive.

Even the youngest students should have procedures for putting away manipulatives and supplies independently. When I taught first grade, I printed out photos of how things fit in the cupboards and posted them on the appropriate walls. Don't underestimate what students can do, even if they don't do it precisely to your standard of perfection.

Capitalize on Your Biology

Some of us pop out of bed like a piece of toast in the morning. We're energized, chatty, and ready to take on our day. Others need to flirt with a pot of coffee for at least an hour before considering talking to others.

While it is natural for a body's energy to fluctuate during the day, people generally fall into the category of either "early birds" who are most productive in the morning or "night owls" who are most productive at the end of the day. While we don't have control over our traditional school hours, we can be strategic about matching tasks that we need to do outside of the classroom to our energy level.

It is helpful to identify our productivity weak spots. This way, we can capitalize on the time that we know we are most likely to be at our peak performance.

I am lucky that I generally wake up energized and optimistic. Over the years, I have consistently stuck to the habit of "eating my problems for breakfast". This means I deal with the most disagreeable or least preferred tasks first thing in the morning.

By doing this, I can feel immediately productive. I'm someone who tends to overthink different scenarios and conversations that haven't happened yet. When I procrastinate on talking with a disgruntled parent or dealing with an unpleasant email, I find I waste too much emotional energy during the day. It's as if the task hangs over my head, and I'll spend more time worrying about it, talking about it, and avoiding it, than it would actually take to just take care of it. So for me, it'll always be the first thing I get done. By the late afternoon, and certainly in the evening, I'm usually tired and more easily irritated.

But that's me. If you know you are not a morning person and are more likely to be a little crabby or defensive in the morning, be strategic about scheduling your difficult work later in the day.

Research in the science of peak performance and motivation points to the fact that different tasks should ideally be synced to our energy level. Analytical tasks are best accomplished when our energy level is high and we are free from distractions and able to focus. When our energy level is lower and our mind is more easily distractible, we will be more productive in working on creative tasks. This is why many times we come up with good ideas when we are walking or relaxing. It's worth investing the energy in determining our natural energy pattern and wherever possible have it work for us, not against us.

Watch Your Mental Diet

When I was a child, one of my favorite candies was sugar cigarettes. They came in a cute cigarette box and even had pink-tipped "filters" on them. I earned them as a special treat if I sat quietly in church on Sunday.

We've evolved past those days. Now we recognize not only are cigarettes harmful but so is the sugar. We know more about the quality of nutrition and differentiate between nutrients that sustain us and those that provide a quick glucose or caffeine energy spike but aren't great for us in the long run.

When we binge on low-quality fast food and put nothing in our bodies but sugar, preservatives, and caffeine, we wouldn't expect our body to feel good or perform at its best. It's the same with our mental diet. Our minds are like fertile soil- what we plant in them grows. The problem is, we're not always mindful about what we're planting.

What we plant in our mind comes in many forms. First, it's the people we spend time with and the conversations we engage in. It's also the books and blogs we read, the music and podcasts we listen to, and the shows we watch on TV. It's the video games and apps we play. Finally, it's social media, and all the comments we allow to influence us in persistent 280 character increments.

Conduct a quick inventory of what you are planting in your mind. Is your teacher crew primarily people who admire problems or people who propose solutions? What do you read, and what do you listen to? What do you comment on? Is it more focused on uplifting and hopeful topics? Is it focused on learning and growing? Or is it all zombie apocalypse, trauma, anger, and stress-inducing?

I am not here to judge anyone's habits. Goodness knows I reveled in the distraction that binge-watching "Tiger King" provided, and the connection and fun that came out of sharing funny memes. But as a general rule, I'm really particular about what I invest my mental energy in.

It's hard to maintain the mindset of living in Einstein's "friendly world" if we are continually watching crime shows, reading conspiracy theories, and engaging in polarizing arguments on social media. Recognize that all news outlets, blogs, and much of what we see on our Facebook feed has an agenda. A little social media or mindless comedy distraction is all good once in a while, like a splurging on a glass of wine or a decadent piece of chocolate cake. But it shouldn't comprise the majority of our diet, or there is no way we can expect to feel good. To reduce stress and feel mentally strong, it's essential to regulate our mental diet as much as we regulate our nutritional one.

A quick word about the teacher lounge. I had one professor only ever refer to the teacher staff room as "the den of iniquity." In my experience, his description wasn't far off.

Many teachers enjoy spending lunch with their colleagues, laughing, planning, and supporting each other. If that's what happens in your staff room, that's great! But many times it's not. There is a legitimate need for teachers to rely on a few trusted colleagues for emotional and practical support and advice. They can help to give perspective and make us laugh at the crazy situations we sometimes find ourselves in.

However, many staff rooms are simply an area for negative and complaining teachers to congregate. Gossip and blame-shifting do not make for good lunch buddies. Spending our limited lunch break in such an environment can not only give us indigestion but leave us feeling more drained and depleted. It can be a very toxic environment.

Simply ask yourself the question:

Do you feel better or worse after spending time in the staff room?

Does it leave you feeling inspired and invigorated, or did you find yourself getting sucked into the vortex of other people's drama and negativity?

One way to gauge if the staff lunchroom is a place to spend time is to examine the tone and content of the conversations. Do they mostly focus on what's going well in classrooms and on campus, or about the students, parents, and other staff members bothering them?

Sometimes it's easier to find just a few like-minded teachers that you enjoy spending time with and schedule that time intentionally. For example, maybe plan on eating lunch together two times a week to chat and relax and dedicate the other three days to having a restful and restorative lunch break by yourself, or even a working lunch.

Be Intentional About Finding Balance

A consistent theme in my work is that if we don't take care of ourselves, it's tough to take care of other people. This is especially true for teachers. Taking care of other people's children not only on an educational but also social and emotional level is essential but exhausting work. Other people's children can't become more important to us than taking care of our families and ourselves.

I love teaching, and I can't imagine my life without it, but it's not my whole life. Finding balance is critical if we want to have a long and rewarding career.

Many times work will be all-consuming. We can expect to work more at the beginning of the year and at the end of the year, during conferences, and certainly when we had to pivot to distance learning. However, giving 100% of our energy to work is not sustainable. Carving out time to take care of ourselves will not happen unless we are strategic and intentional. Waiting to fill up our own tank until everything else is taken care of doesn't work.

There is always more we could be doing. We need to get comfortable with the idea that some things just won't get done to perfection, or maybe not even done at all. And the world will go on.

Since we are talking about time boxes, I advise that at least every couple of days, we schedule some time boxes with our own names. We should reserve this time to engage in activities that replenish us. Consider these sacred commitments that cannot be broken.

Just as we would not blow off a scheduled doctor's appointment or a parent meeting, we should not blow off commitments that we make to ourselves.

Moving beyond the critical areas of eating well, exercising, and sleeping well, consider activities that recharge your spirit and truly connect you to others. Drinking wine or a beer and binge-watching Netflix can be relaxing and distracting, which has its place. But it's not necessarily going to recharge you.

Schedule time, even if it's just virtually, to spend with loved ones and friends who are not teachers. Spend time laughing, crying, or just listening to people who are important to you. Many times our conversations with co-workers and students are purely surface level, either to relay information or confirm learning. There is so much value in deeply connecting with others.

Make sure you do at least one thing that is uniquely for its joy every day, even if just for ten minutes, whether that's drinking your coffee outside whilst watching the birds, writing in a journal, reading something inspirational, or engaging in a creative hobby.

We live in a culture that places a high value on action and achievement, but we don't always need to be productive. Don't underestimate the value of a good nap. Even God rested on the seventh day.

If you read Positive Mindset Habits for Teachers, you might remember the chapter on finding balance while juggling all of our responsibilities. Many teachers have told me that the Wheel of School/Life Balance activity I created has been beneficial. It's a detailed but valuable exercise. I have included the instructions and chart necessary to complete the exercise in the workbook.

If you have done the exercise before, I invite you to revisit it. Our priorities and needs change based on what is happening in our life and our world. This will be especially important for anybody reading this book as we are emerging from an unprecedented worldwide "shelter in place".

$$\sim$$

THESE ARE some of the best ways I have managed to stay energized and excited about teaching and going to work every day. When my little teaching breakdown happened, I needed to be very honest with myself. Was I walking my talk? I am the lady known for writing about positive mindsets, for goodness sake! I felt shame and frustration when admitting to myself that, even though I knew better, I had completely let go of any notion of self-care and proactively reducing overwhelm. I just kept thinking I could power through. Those poor choices, coupled with losing sight of my teaching North Star, led to my "dark night of the soul". In a supply closet. With students lining up outside.

IN THE NEXT CHAPTER, I will reveal the magic nine words I teased you with at the beginning of the book. The nine words that got me off the floor and helped me create the highest level of "vibe" in my classroom. They deal with a topic that is rarely discussed, but that is a significant cause of stress- how to manage our image and the way we are perceived as teachers.

6

Optics Matter

WHEN I WAS 37 years old and in the throes of a mid-life reboot, I quit a successful corporate career and returned to school. I had never even stepped foot on a US college campus, and it had been 16 years since I had last been in a lecture room. I had no idea what to expect.

I remember many things about that first day. Some of them are pretty funny in hindsight. Like how long I agonized about what to wear. What first-day outfit would set the tone that I was serious about learning, yet also hip enough to relate to my young adult classmates? Turns out, there is no such outfit. I looked like some awkward version of their mom trying too hard. To add to the awkwardness, at some point during the day, I had managed to sit in melted chocolate and walked around with a giant brown stain on the back of those neatly pressed corporate casual khakis.

Then there was the parking debacle. While most of my classmates were youngsters who had walked or biked to class, I was almost late because I had to drop off two children at daycare, drive 60 miles to get to campus, and then struggle to park my minivan in the tiny parking spaces marked "sub-compact". Once parked, I realized there wasn't enough room to open the door. I was forced to climb over the back seat and exit out of the rear pop up door, hoping no one would notice.

But here's what I remember most. That was the day I was introduced to the single most useful insight of the teacher credentialing program. In fact, it happened within the first five minutes of my first class. And I may have been the only person in the room who was paying attention.

When Dr. Smith made his entrance into that first class, the room rapidly hushed. A middle-aged man dressed in a well-worn suit and a bow tie, Dr. Smith had a thick accent from Ghana and looked even more out of place than me. His opening remarks about the great responsibility of spending our days with, "udder people's children" elicited several snickers. By the time he listed his credentials, which included teaching overseas and at an American military school, "where students didn't show up in their slippers", most of the room seemed to have written him off as an eccentric fellow whose mandatory class in Cross Cultural Language Acquisition was going to be a drag.

To be honest, Dr. Smith's instructional plan for the next 13 weeks was pretty uninspiring. He divided the class into ten groups and assigned each a chapter of a book to report back on. A basic "jigsaw" strategy we had all been aware of since middle school. For the next ten weeks, he did nothing but nod at the tedious slides we presented.

For someone like me, commuting 100 plus miles a day round trip to get to campus, it would have been easier to just read the book at home and save on time and gas. I don't even recall what we did in those last two weeks of class. Probably a multiple-choice final on a Scantron sheet so that he wouldn't have to grade it.

The insight was not that if you are merely "going through the motions" as a teacher, your students can tell, although it was good to learn early on in the program. Dr. Smith's pearl of wisdom that has sustained me for 18 years in the classroom was this:

"When I close my door, I become a revolutionary."

Dr. Smith

Let me give these words some context.

Dr. Smith explained that in his thirty years of teaching experience, there had rarely been anything "new" in education. He proposed that many educational initiatives were simply old concepts with new acronyms and that certain educational "fads" go in cycles. For example, the debate about explicit instruction of phonics versus whole language learning in primary grades. He said that for many years he sat in meetings where he was given new procedures, new mandates, new forms to complete and many other directives that were simply too numerous to implement, all the while knowing they would be quickly forgotten the following year.

At the time, I couldn't relate, but now I recognize that as a pretty universal "professional development day" scenario.

What struck me was his extraordinarily calm and pleasant demeanor when he explained his best advice for dealing with this. "I just smile and nod my head. Yes, sir. Yes, sir. Yes, sir." And then, with a twinkle in his eye, he looked right at me and said, "And then when I close my door, I become a revolutionary."

I didn't have the language to articulate what he meant back then. But I absolutely understood what he was saying. He was talking about his teaching North Star. Sit politely in the meetings. Don't argue or cause waves or draw attention to yourself. Be open to new ideas and growing, of course. But when you go back to your room, give students what you know they need to learn. Be a revolutionary.

I'm not suggesting that blatant acts of subversion will make you a better teacher. Of the many "new programs" I have been introduced to over the years, most of them had some excellent information that I started using. I subscribe to the idea of "take what you need and leave the rest." But don't become unduly stressed. If something really seems "off" and you have a strong objection, quietly talk with your admin about it. If not, just let it go. When you get to your room, put the poster on the wall. Learn the new acronyms. And then tune out all the noise, all of the latest jargon, and get on with the real business of giving other people's children the help and support they need.

Don't risk being perceived as not being on board. Learn to play the game.

Why is it important to play the game?

The short answer is because people judge. How you are perceived as a teacher matters. Administrators, school board members, parents, and even colleagues often judge us on superficial appearances and not truly important criteria such as class vibe or student-centered metrics.

It's not right, and it's not fair. But it is what we deal with every day. It's easier to accept this fact and be smart about proactively managing the "optics" of how we are perceived. It will save us a lot of grief and stress in the long run. It will allow us to be left alone to do our best teaching.

In researching this quote, it was attributed to numerous people.

"You can please all of the people some of the time. You can please some of the people all of the time. But you can't please all of the people all of the time."

Although I can't guarantee who originally said it, I can guarantee they weren't a teacher.

There are plenty of times where it seems like there is no way to please all the stakeholders, especially parents. While I'm not suggesting pleasing all the parents is necessary or even advisable, the fact remains that the less friction you have with parents, the less stressed you'll feel and the more productive you can be. You can reserve your energy to do the necessary work of teaching children.

Being judged by parents is not a new problem.

In my third grade class, we visit a historic one-room pioneer school-house and reenacted a day of school in 1886. One of the ways I prepare my students is to watch an episode of Little House on the Prairie called "Schoolhouse Mom". Little House on the Prairie was a popular TV show in the 1970s and is based on the Little House in the Big Woods book series by Laura Ingalls Wilder. The students loved to see the costumes and were fascinated by students of all ages having just one teacher. When we visited the school, they laughed at the long list of "Rules for Teachers" posted. It listed the many things teachers are and are not allowed to do in public.

Anyway, in this particular episode, Mrs. Ingalls teaches school when the regular school mistress gets injured. Her neighbor, Mrs. Olsen, starts spreading rumors and questioning Mrs. Ingalls's credentials and teaching methods. She's jealous of the positive attention Mrs. Ingalls is receiving. Mrs. Olsen is frustrated that she won't give her children preferential treatment in class, even though Mrs. Olsen is on the equivalent of the school board. She tries to get others stirred up against Mrs. Ingalls for a while and even succeeds in having her step down.

It seems living in a fishbowl and being held up to very high standards is nothing new, except that in modern times, we have better technology. Parents don't even need to assemble in the parking lot anymore. They can openly criticize us from the comfort of their phones on social media groups and private texting. I make it a habit to never look at our school Facebook page. Our administrator refers to some parents on there as the "Facebook Mafia". Why would I voluntarily ingest that kind of negativity into my mental diet?

Unfortunately, I've known some good teachers who were so bullied by parents that they quit. I've also known more than one untenured teacher targeted by "high profile" parents and fired to appease them.

Obviously, the best thing we can do to protect ourselves from parental criticism is to make sure that children are happy spending their day with us and that they are learning and succeeding. But given how much stress this can all cause, it's also advisable to take a few proactive measures to manage how we are perceived.

Here are some suggestions on how to do this:

Make Some Deposits

Remember the emotional bank accounts? One of the best ways to establish some goodwill and minimize the likelihood of being criticized is to make plenty of deposits in parent bank accounts early on in the year.

Take the time to make introductory phone calls or send emails as soon as you get your class list. I talked about this in the Back to School section. Get the ball rolling on a positive note.

Model good manners I keep a box of thank you notes in my draw. If a parent goes out of their way to send in extra school supplies, send them a thank you note or a quick email.

Present yourself as an organized professional If you have students with special accommodations or health needs, reach out to the parents ahead of time to let them know you are aware of the situation. They need to feel their child is safe with you. One first day of school, as I was greeting my new students, a parent stood in the doorway and quizzed me about the contents of her son's Individualized Educational Plan. Luckily, I was prepared and tried to encourage her to come by at the end of day to discuss the details with me privately. But it really made me realize how she was not prepared to leave her son in my care unless she was assured I know how to meet his needs. Her concern was real. I should have taken responsibility and reached out to her beforehand.

Remember that first impressions matter You will be judged on what you wear, how you fix your hair, how tidy you keep your room, and how clean your car is—this is sad but true.

My children were in school before I became a teacher. I don't think what I wanted as a parent was unreasonable and probably no different from what most parents want. I wanted to know that my children were with a qualified, competent, organized teacher who cared for students. I wanted my children to be treated fairly and kindly. I wanted to have confidence that when issues of bullying or conflict came up (and they did) that the teacher would take the matter seriously and had the skills to resolve or deescalate the issue. And I wanted to be assured they had high academic expectations for my children and were willing to communicate with me if help was needed holding them accountable.

I don't remember ever emailing or calling a teacher other than to volunteer in the classroom. My children always completed their homework. When field trip money or supplies were required, I often sent in double so that the teacher wouldn't need to use their own money if other parents didn't come through. I even made several handmade quilts for teacher appreciation gifts.

Am I bragging? No, I'm saying that by most standards, I was a good, low-key, supportive parent. And yet I can remember being super judgmental at a Back to School Night presentation where the teacher's room seemed very disorganized. The teacher was scruffy, and she was struggling with the technology for her presentation. It was the first time I met her and had not had any communication with her prior, other than a request for supplies. I was not impressed. Had she made some simple deposits, such as a welcome email or smiling to meet us at the door, I would have been more likely to extend her a little grace.

Once that poor first impression was made, I was more likely to be critical of any small mistake she made.

Common Sense Suggestions

Here's my point. Use common sense to avoid parents and adminis-trators making unfair assumptions about you. Put your best foot forward.

Should it matter if you dress comfortably? No, it shouldn't. But make sure that any time you know parents or admins are coming by or you have a meeting, you are dressed professionally.

Make sure your room is tidy I kept a large empty tote box in my room for many years. Even with just a few minutes' notice someone was coming, I could fill it with my clutter and shove it under my desk. Play the game.

Even if you are tenured and well respected by your administrator, you still need to make an effort to have a perfect room and an engaging learning activity when you are formally observed. I know many admins say, "I don't need a dog and pony show." Even if they don't think they need it, they appreciate seeing you doing your best teaching. Give them the dog and pony show.

Mind who you trust I am a very trusting person. I've repeated in this book several times that it's best for our mental health to assume everyone has good intentions. However, experience has taught me to be a little less naive in this area and pay attention to who I share things with. I have been stabbed in the back more than once by some colleagues and parents. I know my teaching crew. I know who I can trust to hold counsel and to listen to me when I need to vent. Be very careful about being critical of parents, administrative decisions, coworkers, or even students around specific individuals. Some people thrive on drama and try to feel better about themselves by making others look bad. I like to give people the benefit of the doubt, but I have learned the hard way to be a little smarter.

Keep up with posting grades One common cause of parents jumping to the unfair conclusion that teachers are overwhelmed, lazy, or undedicated is the school "parent portal" or digital grade book not being up to date. Ironically, it is usually the students with good grades that have parents all over us about updating the grade book. We would love for the parents of students with declining grades and large amounts of missing assignments to be equally on top of things. But it's important to keep the grade book current. Apart from ensuring we are not harshly judged, it is also unfair for students to be aware of their current grade. No one wants to learn they had poor grades on three or four assignments. That might seem impossible to recover from. If a student or a parent had been aware after one poor grade, maybe they could be more proactive about rectifying the situation.

In the section on time management, I gave suggestions for time boxing. It is helpful to schedule a regular time box for posting grades. As with many things, it's easier to plan and keep up than try and find the time to catch up.

Leverage Technology to Share the Great Things You Are Doing

You know all the wonderful, engaging activities we do in class? We need to be proactive in a non-braggy way about sharing them with parents and administrators.

I remember last year we were learning about forces and motion. I spent hours preparing supplies at home. I borrowed another room's aide so that I could have the help of another adult. For an hour, the students engaged in a hands-on lesson activity making "hoppers" and measuring how high they could launch them. Students were loud, laughing, engaged, collaborating, and learning. The classroom vibe was mildly chaotic.

The next day we engaged in a combination science and PE lesson. The students and I participated in a simulation to see if we could outrun different dinosaurs, based on their stride lengths. When the students realized even I would have been eaten, we all laid on the floor and "played dead" next to the chalk lines of the activity and had an older student take a photo of us. When school was out half an hour later, I was standing right next to a student when the parent picking them up asked, *"What did you do in school today?"* You can guess what the student said? *"Nothing."*

Luckily, I had posted photos of both of those activities to the Class Stories page in Class Dojo. It takes less than 10 seconds to do. An alert goes straight to a parent's phone. Thankfully, the parent called the student out on his lazy answer and showed him one of the photos saying, "Really? Because this looked kind of fun. Tell me about it in the car."

If we don't make an effort to promote what we have been doing, we run the risk that the only things parents hear about us are when we mess up, when we raise our voice, or when someone gets in trouble or throws up in class. I've had children in school and asked what they learned in school that day. I know this for a fact.

When I first started teaching, I would send home a weekly class newsletter. I would describe all the things we were learning and any calendar items etc. Weeks later, I would often find those newsletters scrunched up in the bottom of backpacks along with half-eaten lunches. When technology improved, I created a class web page providing one-stop shopping for homework assignments, class information, and photos of our fun activities. It took a lot of time and hardly anyone ever looked at it. Now the technology is easy and convenient. It's in our pocket.

Whatever your preferred parent communication tool is, it likely has a Class Stories type feature. It's a stream where the teacher can post photos, captions, and short videos. I take the photos directly on the app so that there is no weirdness about having pictures of students on my personal phone. The notification goes straight to the parent's phone, and I can even see who has viewed it - most parents do!

I would have loved to have received pictures of my child at school, engaged in PE, or a hands-on math activity. I make sure I send 2-3 photos a week. Not more. Some parents who can't make it to awards assemblies will ask me to snap a photo and send it to them. I am always happy to oblige. I was the working mom who could never participate in school activities with my children. It's a nice low-key way of letting parents know that their child is in an engaging and academically challenging environment, because we can't rely on all of the students to be bragging about us!

Once in a while, post some pictures to your school's Facebook page so that your administrator can see the fun, too. Don't be the teacher who posts all the time, or you can be perceived as being boastful or maybe even insecure about your teaching as if you need to solicit likes and feedback for validation. But find the balance.

Don't Self Sabotage on Social Media

Here are a few thoughts about Facebook and other social media sites. I teach students early on that nothing they post on the internet ever disappears. Even if they think they have erased or deleted it, it can still be found. Now, I don't expect any of us to have computer forensic experts ever seize our laptops. But it's best to proceed with the same level of caution when engaging in social media.

Again, use common sense. Most schools will prohibit you from being connected on social media with students. But what about parents? It's really awkward to decline a friend request from a parent. But I'm recommending you do so. Refer back to my previous comment about being mindful about who you trust.

Maybe consider having two accounts—one for "school" and one for personal use. But even if you use a maiden name or alias, it's easy for people to find your Facebook account if you comment on a colleague's stream or they "tag" you. If they've friended a parent, you have been outed.

Use good judgment about what you post. Avoid sharing polarizing or controversial political posts. Your "friends" know where you stand on most issues, anyway. Be mindful of the photos you post. Are you partying hard in every single one? Are you posting anything that could put the school district in a potentially uncomfortable position?

I know that what you choose to do outside of work hours should not be anybody's business, but the internet has made it very easy for it to be everybody's business. I know strong teacher candidates who did not get job offers based on their Facebook feeds. Yes, that's possible grounds for litigation, and it certainly wasn't the reason they were given for not being hired. But be mindful, nonetheless. Consider how many news stories are about people who have lost their jobs or product endorsement income because of something they have said on social media. This is the world we live in.

Be Strategic About Being Seen and Known

When discussing volunteering for adjunct duties, I made the recommendation that if you are new in a school or a district, you should be strategic about being seen and heard by the right people. Even if you are not new, do the school board members know who you are? I make it a point to go to at least one school board meeting a quarter, even if I don't stay the entire time. It can never hurt to be seen and known.

Most teachers rely heavily on funds raised by parent groups. If you are not known by the parents, it's a good idea to participate in the fundraising meetings and to be seen volunteering at events. Get into the habit of sending thank you emails or having your class write thank you letters after events. If you buy classroom supplies, send pictures of the students using them. If you go on a field trip with fundraised money, again, make sure you take photos and that students write a thank you.

These are basic good manners and ensure that you are making deposits in your relationship with the parent club, not just withdrawals.

Wear the Darn Mask

My sincere hope is that by the time you read this book wearing masks will have gone the way of fidget spinners - something really annoying that we had to deal with, but that suddenly went away. But my suspicion is that they won't.

Just as children can't learn if they don't feel safe, parents will have a hard time assuming the best intentions of us and extending us grace if they don't feel their children are safe at school. Regardless of your personal opinion on the matter, if your school decides all school personnel need to wear masks, be sure not to be caught without one. Not after school in the parking lot. Not when you are crossing campus after students have left. Wearing masks has become a very polarizing issue. Please don't become a victim of a social media witch hunt when parents start shaming teachers who are caught not wearing masks on campus.

~

I HOPE these suggestions have come across in the spirit I have intended. I don't believe that I am a deceitful person who feels and acts one way in private while portraying a different face in public. If I weren't totally transparent, I would undoubtedly write different types of books. I was successful in the business world for many years. Managing optics in the business world is called being "politically savvy", and I see it lacking on quite a few campuses. It just means be aware of how you are perceived.

Education needs vocal activists. If you are passionate about fighting for teacher rights, take on a role with the teacher's union. I really admire colleagues who do so and acknowledge that my work life is better due to their efforts.

But that's not my path. I'm more of a foot soldier and cheerleader. My desire has only ever been to be in the classroom, with my students, teaching, learning, supporting each other, and having fun.

By flying under the radar, by delivering results while proactively pleasing the appropriate stakeholders, I do just that without much drama. But when I close my door...I let my teaching North Star guide me, and I become a revolutionary.

Afterward

Conventional wisdom of non-fiction books dictates that I should write chapter summaries in the conclusion. I opted for a detailed table of comments at the beginning. I trust you spend enough time with text features to know how to find whatever interests you in here. I won't waste your time by repeating it.

However, this last page is valuable real estate, and there is something that I want to repeat. Teaching in the classrooms of the future when so much is uncertain and rapidly changing is going to be challenging. But we are capable.

Educating the hearts and minds of students is a high stakes endeavor. Our futures and that of our children are dependent on the outcome. If we're strategic and intentional, we can write our own narrative, despite the challenges. Our experience of teaching can be rewarding and fulfilling, as well as necessary.

For the length of this book, you have been my student, so I leave you with this:

- I see you.
- You matter.
- You are safe here.
- I believe that you can achieve great things.
- Your success is important to me.

We got this.

Grace

Additional Resources

TED TALKS REFERENCED IN THE BOOK:

Alan November : What is the Value of a Teacher

Click Here

Rita Pierson : Every Kid needs a Champion

Click Here

SECTION 1

Mindset: The New Psychology of Success – Carol Dweck

The Happiness Advantage: How a Positive Brain Fuels Success in Work and Life - Shawn Achor

Happy Teachers Change the World – A Guide to Mindfulness in Education - Thich Nhat Hanh and Katherine Weare

SECTION 2

The First Days of School: How to Be an Effective Teacher - Harry K. Wong and Rosemary T. Wong

The Seven Habits of Highly Effective People - Steven Covey

Setting Limits in the Classroom - Robert MacKenzie

Teaching with Love and Logic: Taking Control of the Classroom - Jim Fay And David Funk

Restorative Justice Handbook for Teachers, Disciplinarians and Administrators - Bob Costello and Joshua Wachtel

For information on Positive Behavior Intervention Support

https://www.pbis.org/

For resources on social/emotional learning

https://www.commonsense.org/education/toolkit/social-emotional-learning

SECTION 3

Flow: The Psychology of Optimal Experience- Mihaly Csikszentmihalyi

To learn more about the Pomodoro Technique visit :

http://pomodorotechnique.com/

ADDITIONAL RESOURCES FOR E-LEARNING

https://www.iste.org/ - International Society for Technology in Education

https://www.commonsense.org/education/

Help Teachers You've Never Met

If you enjoyed this book and found it useful, it would mean the world to me if you would leave a REVIEW on Amazon. It doesn't need to be a writing assignment, just a few sentences about what you liked about the book and who might find it helpful. You can leave a review even if the book was given to you as a gift or for Professional Development.

Every review counts, and helps this book find its way to people who may need to hear a message of hope for teaching in these challenging times.

~

About the Author

Grace Stevens abandoned a successful corporate VP career in 2001 to become a public school teacher, and she has never been happier. She is a Certified NLP (Neuro-Linguistic Programming) Practitioner, a closet nerd, and author of the One New Habit Book Series, and the bestselling Positive Mindset Habit for Teachers. Having lived and studied in four countries, she settled in N. California where she raised her family and teaches elementary school. Her mission is simple - happier classrooms for teachers and students.

f

You May Also Love

Want to put more joy in your classroom and your life?

A quick read in a conversational tone, this best-selling book will help put a *smile* back on your face and *laughter* back in your classroom - two essential elements for teacher fulfillment and student success.

Praise for Positive Mindset Habits for Teachers

"Great Read!!!! This book gives readers awesome insight into teaching and how to have a positive mindset for teachers. It feels like you're having a good conversation with a fellow teacher making it relatable and easy to follow. If you're looking for an honest book about teaching that you can actually learn real skills to use in the classroom, this is it."

Amazon ***** Review

"Just what I needed as a teacher of 20 years. Great strategies for new teachers as well as reminders for the veterans. If you are new to the classroom or feeling burnt out, I really recommend this book!" -

Amazon ***** Review

Made in the USA
Middletown, DE
17 November 2020